Nobody Cares and What I Did About It!

The Red Wemette Story of The Chicago Outfit

Red Wemette

NOBODY CARES AND WHAT I DID ABOUT IT!
THE RED WEMETTE STORY OF
THE CHICAGO OUTFIT

RED WEMETTE

Digital Publishing of Florida, Inc.
Book Printing for the Author and Publisher
www.digitaldata-corp.com

ISBN 13-Digit: 978-1-942634-50-8

Credits: Cover Image by pigprox.
         All interior images from Red Wemette

Disclaimer:

This book is designed to provide information about the subject matter covered. The opinions and information expressed in this book are those of the author, not the publisher. Every effort has been made to make this book as complete and as accurate as possible. However, there may be mistakes both typographical and in content. Therefore, this text should be used only as a general guide and not as the ultimate source of information. The author and publisher of this book shall have neither liability nor responsibility to any person or entity with respect to any loss or damage caused or alleged to be caused directly or indirectly by the information contained in this book.

Printed in the United States of America

DEDICATION

This book is dedicated to all of the victims of organized crime and their families. And to the private citizens and people who have the courage to come forward and help law enforcement, on every level, to bring criminals to justice. Even if that means that you are not politically correct in reporting potential perpetrators to the proper authorities—especially when our freedoms are at risk.

God bless you, one and all.

-Red

Nobody Cares and What I Did About It!

This City is what it is because our citizens are what they are.
-Plato

This is the story of a young man that wanted to make Chicago a safer place for people who had their lives changed, for the worse, by Chicago's Italian run Outfit. There are many names for the organized criminal underground. Their trademarks of extortion, murder, gambling, and their rackets that spread from Chicago to the Pacific Ocean—and every city in between—are their crime family's line of business. At the time of these events, it was the largest criminal enterprise in the United States. Unlike the five New York families that fought with each other over their turf, the Chicago mob kept control of their ranks and crews as they expanded operations like true opportunists. These guys were literally getting away with murder, and I felt—and do still feel—that I could and did make a difference.

In August of 1971, I contacted special agent John Osborne of the Federal Bureau of Investigation: not to make a deal, not because I was in trouble, but because I saw the FBI knocking on doors asking questions about crime bosses that ran operations in the area. No one would talk to them. They knew that if they did speak up, they could be murdered, or at the very least, be out of a job.

During that time in my life I worked as a bartender at one of the many Outfit taverns that were common in Chicago. I had the duty of giving an envelope of money, once a week, to the Chicago Police as part of a payoff to make sure they didn't come around if they were called. I was also responsible for serving drinks to people from all walks of life. The Outfit liked to handle things in their own way, with or without the police.

I am William "Red" Wemette and this is my story.

TABLE OF CONTENTS

TABLE OF CONTENTS (CONT)

A Precedent is Set

I suppose you could say that I got an early introduction to life undercover. When I was fifteen years old, I had a job at the Thrift Town department store, a chain that was owned by the Kroger Company, in Moline, Illinois. I worked as the sales manager of the sporting goods department because they were short on help. My dad made an agreement with the store manager, Gene Barr, to help get me the position. Dad was the pharmacy manager of SuperX Drugs, which was also owned by Kroger, and housed in the same building at the end of the strip mall.

Gene treated me extra special, and I never knew why. It kind of confused me. After a few weeks, I noticed that in the evening hours one of the department managers was taking out carpeting through the back delivery doors. He had a few of the stock boys help him take it out. I wondered why it wasn't heading out the front doors like other merchandise. The fact that it also took place at night made it seem odd to me—and I went to Gene about it. He told me not to worry about it. He told me it was an employee purchase, and they were getting off from work at that time and going home. I could see he thought I was very naive and easy to manipulate, but I knew that there was something fishy about his explanation but I left it at that. I went back to my department and got back to work helping customers.

The following day, I was approached by another manager from the electronics department. He told me that if I wanted anything from his department, then I would get an "employee discount" as he winked at me. Later on, I learned that every department manager was stealing from the store—and Gene knew about each one of their thefts!

We had several strange meetings with all the department managers. Gene was always present and they would talk about "shrinkage" as they accounted for transactions and store inventory. There were a lot of discussions about how to account to the district manager for the shortage of inventory and cash money. Sometimes they asked me about my department and then excused me from the meeting as they continued with other topics. I thought that behavior was odd, too, but I just went with the flow and kept busy with my own responsibilities.

The stores of that time period didn't accept credit cards so all transactions were done in cash. I had to account for the sporting goods department's daily earnings and turn over the cash with the cash register's journal to Gene before I left for home each evening. I learned a lot about how retail sales worked. My figures were always between a few cents to two or three dollars off between the cash I returned and the register's journal entries. My sporting goods department hadn't been making more than one hundred dollars a day prior to my taking over. I had turned things around there, and we typically sold between five and seven-hundred dollars of inventory each day—and the daily discrepancy bothered me. Gene told me not to worry about it because only an embezzling employee would show an exact match on the balance sheets and cash intake. As long as it wasn't more than a few bucks, everything was fine.

Part of my duties included drilling custom finger holes when customers bought a bowling ball. It was an elaborate process to fit their hand to the ball and properly drill it. I also used a punch to engrave their names or initials. I got very good at it and never made any mistakes. The back of the store was littered with a number of balls that former employees had messed up, but I simply didn't have that problem. A lot of profit came from that operation, and I took in at least $100 a day in bowling ball sales alone. They even took out adds in the local newspaper with coupon vouchers for bowling deals in my department.

I had been an avid bowler since I was age nine. I had even been a "pin set" boy where I used to make ten cents a rack plus tips—if I did a good job or got lucky and worked a tournament. I always wanted my own bowling ball.

We sold a lot of different colored swirled balls and basic black ones. But I had my eye on the flashiest ball in the store, which just happened to also be the most expensive one. It was a Brunswick Gold Crown. I went to the store manager, Gene, and asked what it would cost me with my employee discount.

"You've been doing such a fine job, son, just go ahead and take it for yourself. We can account for it with all of the mis-drilled balls in the back."

It was just before Christmas. We were slow that night so I went right back and picked out my ball and drilled it for my hand. I also picked out a nice, tan and brown-striped leather bowling bag, which I paid for and rang up on the register. I punched my initials into it, "W.R.W." I then filled it with a light yellow-gold rouge. It was supposed to dry for 24 hours but I was so pleased with myself and so excited that I couldn't wait to get it home. I carefully covered it with brown wrapping paper and put it into the new leather bag, making sure the initials were facing up and would dry as they should. I was on cloud nine as I carried it home.

When I came into the door of our home, I took off my galoshes and put them into the shoe caddy. I placed my ball and bag next it, by the front door. It was snowy that day, and I also had to remove my shoes.

I went to wash my hands before supper.

My mother called my father, sister, and I in to eat. We all sat down at the kitchen table. As was customary in my family, we were discussing the day's activities. My father asked me about the bowling ball. I told him how nice Gene, my boss, was and how he'd given me the ball for nothing because I was doing such a great job for him. I had only had to buy the bag.

He told me, "We'll have to see Gene about that tomorrow."

"All of the department managers are getting employee discounts, Dad." I replied, rather nonchalantly.

When my dad heard that, he dropped his fork. I heard it hit his plate as his mouth went agape and a quizzical expression took over his face. Nothing more was said at the kitchen table after that exchange, and I thought he was angry with me. We finished eating, and my father went into the living room while the rest of us took care of the dishes.

"Come in here, Redhead, and explain this to me."

I went into the room and asked him, "What do ya wanna know, dad?"

I told him about how all of the other department managers had gotten deals on different merchandise. I thought it was just reward for all of the hard work I'd done in bringing up sales in my department. My dad explained that he wasn't mad at me and not to say anything to anybody at the store about anything—and to just act normal. He then got on the phone and called information for Kroger's Cincinnatti headquarters' security office. My mom mentioned something about the cost of long distance.

"Don't worry about it honey. This call is going to pay for itself!"

He stayed on the phone and asked me different questions as he talked things over with a man from Kroger's security. I heard his side of the conversation as he told them how Gene had been borrowing money from the drugstore during their audits in amounts around the eighty to ninety-thousand-dollar range and then returned the cash back to the pharmacy. Kroger security decided to set up a sting operation and told my dad how they would proceed. He was not to loan Gene money the next time during a surprise audit and to tell him that he'd already made the deposit if he came asking for it. The details were worked out over the next hour of conversation, and I did my homework on the kitchen table before we all went to bed for the night.

Two days later, the security team showed up. There were two types of people who comprised the team: two small bookkeepers with glasses who performed the actual audits and eight large men who looked like they ate nails for breakfast and could've been starting linebackers for the NFL. Despite their intimidating appearance, they were very neatly groomed and very professional in their demeanor. They arrived before the store opened, and it was clear to me that somebody was in trouble.

I saw Gene wearing a pair of dark sunglasses that concealed his eyes as he returned from my dad's pharmacy with a desperate look on his face. That was the first time I had ever seen him in sunglasses. I caught a glimpse of his red, puffy eyes as he appeared to wipe a tear from the right corner of his eye, just above his cheek. The team took over the store and roped off the staircase that led to the managing employees' offices. Gene was the first one they met with, and he didn't have a chance to discuss anything with any of the other managers before they whisked him upstairs for interrogation. Throughout the remainder of the day, each department manager got a turn, one at a time. I made a few trips to the snack bar that was one floor beneath that office. I heard a lot of banging around and loud exchanges, but I couldn't quite make out specific words.

Sometime later, Mr. Tippet, the department manager over carpet and other home goods, came out from the offices and looked like he had been ruffed up. His shirt was torn and the top button was missing, his tie was gone, and his arms were red. I could see a bruise mark near his collarbone. I must have been staring at him as he descended the staircase. He rather sarcastically and threateningly told me, "Just wait til you get up there! Yer gonna wind up dead if you say anything!"

I was scared and wanted to call my dad—but I couldn't leave. My turn to ascend the staircase finally came. I unwillingly made my way to the main office, not knowing what was going to happen, and wondering if they were going to beat me up, too.

As I came into the office, the head of security told me to sit down and asked me if I wanted a soda. He was very relaxed and calm. I could tell that he was trying to make me feel comfortable. He then explained to me that I would be sitting there for several hours and that I didn't need to give him any information, as my dad had already told him about me. I was relieved. I figured it was the very man that my father had spoken with on the phone. He was wearing a nice suit and tie. He just spoke to me about normal, everyday things that had nothing to do with the store. We talked about my schooling, hobbies and interests, and he even asked me if I was a good bowler. Before I left, he cautioned me not to talk to any of the other managers, and that if anyone should ask me about what happened to me, then I was to simply reply, "I can't talk about it."

As I left the office and made my way downstairs, I was passed by another department head. We didn't say anything to each other. I went back to helping customers and finished a normal day's operations before finally heading home at the end of my shift.

When I arrived home I was surprised to see that my dad was already home. He was telling my mother, "Call the movers! We are moving back to Chicago!" He further explained that he would be managing the largest SuperX pharmacy in the chain and that it was under construction at Ford City in Chicago. At that time, Ford City was advertised on TV as "the largest shopping center in the U.S. under one roof." Adding to the surprise, he said that he was getting a large reward and that all of our expenses would be paid by Kroger.

Gene Barr fled the state to Owensboro, Kentucky, but he was arrested later and charged with Grand Larceny and Embezzlement. Authorities caught up with the other department managers on the take, and they were also arrested. That group included Mr. Tippet—the first in what has become a long line of men who threatened my life.

It wasn't long before we had packed up and moved to Cicero, Illinois. My dad took over managing the pharmacy at Ford City and bought himself a brand new Oldsmobile, loaded with all the options. Those options included electric windows, air conditioning, and power steering—things we had never seen, as a family.

My dad later commended me while driving in the car, saying, "None of this would ever have happened if it weren't for you, Redhead." He smiled and seemed very proud of our accomplishment.

I didn't think much about it as I was now focused on my new school and life in Cicero. After all, living in Cicero was a bit of a culture shock for me as I got used to the Italian-run neighborhood. Little did I know that I would later be consorting with organized crime figures. My associations in that area would help me understand how things really worked in Chicago.

HISTORIC TIME LINE

1964: Moline, Illinois and my first undercover job.

Early Summer of 1968: Discharge from Marine Corp and went to Curtis Hansen's Y.A.K. for work.

Early Fall of 1968: Met Ken Hansen and left employ of Curtis.

1969: Tending bar at B-Girl bars, eye opening experiences on Outfit operations and police shakedowns. Worked with Curt, met Jimmy Catuara, transporter trip to Las Vegas, spent time with both Hansen brothers making arrangements for opening my own bookstore, bought 6-flat on Carmen.

1970: Became more acquainted with Chicago Horse Mafia activities, George Jayne's murder.

1971: Contacted the FBI and met with them for the first time. Went to American Bonding with Curt. Met Joey Lombardo (JL), Tony Spilotro, Irv Weiner, Frank Schweihs, Pat Ricciardi, Joey Cossantino, and other "made guys."

1972-3: Driving around and doing Hansen errands.

1973: Northwestern Memorial Hospital visit for panic attacks.

1974: Met Caifano, Johnny Rodgers, and many others while building/constructing store; bought house on Richmond and sold 6-flat. August 30th Labor Day opening weekend for store. Tony Spilotro goes to Vegas with his own crew in order to take over. The store was mine as Curt is told to leave me alone, and I partner with Marshall Caifano. Met Jimmy Cozzo, Phil Amato, Dick Hoyt, Larry and Joey Pettit, Vince Salano, Louie Eboli, and others.

1974-1976: Ran store and created RUSH. Bought out Barry from the bar. Bob Hugel went into witness protection. I met with Hank Schmitt (FBI) 2nd handler. October 1975 liquor license expired.

1976: Grand Stand & Premier off-track betting parlors. JL becomes street boss. Paul Gonsky murder.

1977: Bought out Johnny Roger's part of business, factory take over and RUSH production ceases. Joseph "Little Caesar" DeVarco's arrest. Mayor Daley died. Ray Ryan murder.

1978: Jimmy Catuara's murder [July]. Dave Daruse story. Sonny became my bodyguard. Richard Bernouski's murder.

1979: Marshall busted for Westinghouse Stock; great snowstorm in Chicago; Jane Byrne elected.

1981: Purchased the tavern building from Jay Corbett. Moved to Wells Street. Joey held the meeting and charged Frank with taking care of me. Frank went to Florida.

1982: MCRA video machines purchased to replace 8mm with VCRs on monochrome monitors and switched to tokens from the Green Duck in Tennessee for Chicago's Old Town Video.

1983: Joker Poker machines for the tavern. Phil Amato stops collecting from me. I was introduced to Jeeps who did collections for Louie the Mooch.

1984: Mail order business opened at store, and Toushin put on the muscle.

1985: Purchased Book Store building from Mary O'Keefe; built apartment on Well's Street. Frank's murder of Pat Ricciardi.

1986: Frank returned from Florida and decided to take over all porn by plotting to murder Steve Toushin. Met with Tom Knight and decided on Frank as the target; installed video-taping equipment and began taping Jeeps and Frank.

1987: Don Aronow killed by Frank. Medication makes me mobile again. I go on vacation and buy a house in warm climate and sell off everything.

1988: The Arrest of Frank Schweihs. I pull the plug and leave Chicago.

1993: Met with ATF agents for Kenneth Hansen case.

1994: Continued investigations of Schuessler/Peterson murders.

1995: Kenneth Hansen triple homicide trial.

2000: Appeal for Kenneth Hansen trial granted.

2002: Second trial of Ken Hansen.

2002: Mitch Mars meeting and discussions of a trial for Outfit and use of my video tapes.

2003-5: Ongoing investigations and arrests for Operation Family Secrets.

2007: Family Secrets Trial and resulting convictions of all defendants.

2008: Mitchell Mars dies of lung cancer.

1966 Marine Corp Graduation Photo

How It All Started

Back in 1968, when I was discharged from the Marine Corps, I made an effort to reach out to my uncle, Roy Wemette, my father's brother. As a kid I was forbidden to talk to him, and I always wondered why. He was a taxi driver that worked the streets in the city of Chicago and was a full blown, hard-core alcoholic.

When I found him he was living with a woman named Marion McGann, who was a good-looking, very nice woman. I often wondered what she saw in him. She lived at 5056 N. Claremont on Chicago's north side which is where we met. After a few hours of chat and getting-to-know-you time with Marion, she asked me where I was going to work. I told her I didn't have a job just yet.

She picked up the telephone to call her brother, Curtis Hansen, collect. She did what was then known as a "person-to-person call," telling the operator the call was to Marion. That way, Curt would know who the call was from, and he would decline to accept the charges so the operator would end it. He would then immediately call her back, and as he had an unlimited long distance call pack, it kept Marion from having to pay for the call. This was her way of contacting Curt.

While waiting for Curt's return call to come through, she said, "You have a job now, if you can drive me and your uncle out to my brother's place in Frankfort [Illinois]." Her phone rang, she picked it up and spoke to Curt with some basic small talk before she said, "By the way, I'm coming out for the weekend, and you're giving Roy's nephew a job!"

Marion very casually and matter-of-factly orchestrated our futures, all while she delicately puffed on a cigarette. I could tell that she was a force

Boot-Camp-Clothing-Issue-USMC-1966

to be reckoned with, and I had to admire her example of genuine authority, despite her lack of physical prowess.

It wasn't long before we were loaded in my black 1962 4-door Chevy Bel Air that my mother had given me, and headed out to the Valley View YAK. The Y.A.K. stood for "Young Adults Klub."

On the drive there, Marion told me about her brother. He was a World War II hero that had served our country in the Marine Corps. He was twice decorated with a Silver Star at the battle of Iwo Jima and had a host of other decorations that distinguished him as a real stand out guy for the Corps. He was also a bail bondsman who had a lot of connections with the police in Chicago itself and some of its suburbs.

Uncle Roy told me, as we stopped for gas and to get him a pack of Lucky Strikes, "This is one guy you don't fool around with. He kills people!"

I replied, "Now what do you mean by that?"

Uncle Roy continued, "Just don't fool around with him 'cause he's mobbed up and has killed a few people for them." I knew his tone and words were grave and I gave some real consideration to them as we continued the trip.

We got back into my car and headed out to the open road for the YAK. It was about a two-hour drive from Marion's house on the north side of Chicago to Curt's place on U.S. Highway 30, the Lincoln Highway, in Will County onto what we natives call the South Side. The club was about a mile past Frankfort, Illinois.

I came to learn for myself that Marion's brother, Curtis Hansen, was in very fact, a sometimes hit man that worked for Jimmy "The Bomber" Catuara. Curt had a ninety-nine-year lease on a forty acreage piece of land from Marshall Savings and Loan, an Outfit-controlled Savings & Loan that eventually went bust. His lease rate only cost $100. 00 a year!

He acquired the lease one New Year's Eve when the directors held a late night meeting to discuss and make plans to deal with some bad loans that they were trying to collect or write off. They were not overly concerned, as their institution was federally insured, and, naturally, they offered Curt the lease with the hopes of bringing in some real cash from his operations rather than from the terms of payment set within the lease. Curt also acquired eight 24-unit apartment buildings in Chicago Heights. For over five years he collected the rent and never paid a dime on the mortgage before it was seized for non-payment. He had plenty of opportunities in life, but his *I don't care attitude* let them fall to the wayside.

The YAK property included a luxurious six-bedroom brick house, an extremely large swimming pool, a band shell out in the grove area, a motel that had a converted barn for residences, and an actual barn with several horses for paying guests to ride at their leisure. The large, converted barn was a place for general entertainment but was particularly staged for the teenage crowds. We called it "The Juice Club" because Curt couldn't get a liquor license and that was his next-best alternative. It had a tiered seating arrangement made out of plywood covered in blue shag carpet.

Curt's original idea was to have a nightclub there, but you just can't have a real nightclub without the ability to offer alcoholic beverages. The house was going to be a roadhouse—AKA brothel—with several prostitutes there, but Curt's plans all changed when he took over the property. He got a county license and a state license only to discover that the Feds had their eye on him so he couldn't procure any kind of federal liquor license, despite his best efforts. He was under too much scrutiny to engage in the illicit but profitable activities that he and his cohorts wanted so he had to settle on the next best options, out there in Frankfort, Illinois.

First Impressions

When we finally arrived, I met Curt for the first time. He was a fat man who seemed to be very jolly. He hugged his sister and said hello to me as his sister asked him, "What room will Billy be sleeping in, so he can bring his bags?"

He asked Douggie, a good-looking 19-year-old kid that served as the pool's lifeguard to show me to my room. After I put my duffel bag and clothes away, I joined the rest of the family.

"Go on in and take a look at the kitchen and while you are at it, bring me back a cup of coffee," Curt told me.

As I reviewed the YAK's commercial kitchen, I was simply overwhelmed. I had seen mess halls in the Marine Corps, but nothing like this! It was complete with a walk-in freezer stocked with an array of premium quality steaks, chops, briskets, roasts, fillets, and every other choice cut you can imagine. He had concession fare, too: hot dogs, Italian sausages, Polish sausages, case after case of hamburger patties, boxes and bags of French fries, and every other popular menu item that is common at fairs or carnivals. The walk-in cooler was for milk, butter, and other assorted foods. There was a pantry full of condiments, non-perishables, and serving items for the concession stands. There was also an over-abundance of breakfast foods: cases of eggs, boxes of ham slices, shrink-wrapped cases of bacon, and breads for every type of meal you could need. He had a Hobart eighteen gallon mixer for large dough recipes, huge commercial ovens with stackable baking racks, and a grill that was three-feet deep by eight-feet wide with huge ventilators to help keep smoke out of the air when things really got busy or when the several deep fat fryers got hot and greasy.

I was very impressed as there were thousands of dollars of food that could literally feed hundreds of people, all at a moment's notice. It was a legitimate, professional kitchen.

Curt had told me to look around, and I was really taken in with what I saw. He then told me to make anything I wanted to eat and to cook for anyone else there who wanted food, treating me as his employee right from the get go. I went to get his cup of coffee that flowed from a spigot at the base of an industrial-sized coffee urn. I asked him how he wanted it, and he told me, "Black!" He hollered over his shoulder while he sat at a table with a five-line phone system on it that doubled as his work desk.

We ate our fill and then stayed up late, talking, while Curt just sat at his table and said goodnight as each of the rest of us went to bed. It seemed that Curt never slept.

The next day I woke to Douggie telling me to put my swim trunks on and join everyone at the pool. After a brief swim, Marion asked me to make some breakfast for her and my Uncle Roy. I asked Curt if he wanted something, and he told me, "Not right now." I was hungry as I cooked eggs, bacon and toast for them and myself.

I was terribly curious how such a fat man like Curt didn't want anything to eat. I would later find out he was taking phenobarbital that kept him up most nights and days, all in an attempt to lose some of his extra weight.

After bringing the dishes back to the kitchen, I went out to his enormous pool. I noticed a sign that said "Members Only" on the gate as you entered the fenced-in pool. As I passed it, I saw Marion with her long chestnut hair, sunning herself in a lounge chair in a designer swimsuit. My uncle was sitting next to her, fully clothed and taking in the sights.

Her brother Curt was walking around in waist-deep water at the shallow end of the pool with a cigarette on the very tips of his fingers. There were several other young people in the pool, and they were either swimming or diving off of one of the three, multi-level diving boards.

As I looked at Curt, it made me chuckle. He was covered in hair. Hair follicles seemed to cover every exposed inch of his body. It was a black, thick, curly hair that made it hard to see his dark, olive-oil skin. He featured a rough, unshaven face and a mop of long wavy locks on his head that matched the rest of him. His belly was so fat that it hung over his swim trunks. Speaking of his trunks, they were filled with air and floating out around him owing to the fact that it took a lot of swimsuit material to cover a man with such prodigious girth! He was 5' 8" tall, in his late forties, weighed well over three-hundred pounds and was walking very slowly in the water with a big, toothy grin on his face as he tried to keep his balance with the cup of coffee in his other hand.

He usually didn't go out for a swim, but Marion had challenged him about the fact that he owned a pool but never used it himself. In response, he decided to suit up, enter the water, and was now a real spectacle for each of us to behold.

I was an avid swimmer and dove into the water on that blisteringly hot summer day. Later on, Douggie tossed me a towel as I got out of the water to dry off. I was 6' 1" tall and 155 lbs. with a baby face that made me look about five years younger than I actually was. I had bright red, curly hair, blue eyes, and pasty white skin that burned very easily if I got too much exposure to the sun. I dried off my beanpole of a body and got dressed. My Uncle Roy and Marion later returned to the city, borrowing one of Curt's three Cadillacs, and left me at my new employer's establishment.

My New Job and the Set-Up

I stayed at the club for a few months, doing odd jobs, working for room and board, and $25.00 per week. I regularly served coffee to Curt and his friends, cooked meals for anyone he asked me to cater, cared for his horses, and basically did any job that needed doing. I saw many famous national performers play the YAK Club and meeting them was a big deal for me, at the time. The bands and performers who played there are simply too numerous to list by name. Because of his Outfit connections, Curt always got the most popular groups to play the YAK, and they did so at a loss. That was just a necessary stop if they wanted to work any other Mob-affiliated places, like Las Vegas, that raked in the big tour money, so they typically did their best to make the most of it.

I met Curt's wife, Sally, around the first weekend of my stay. She was a tall, slim, and very beautiful young lady of about twenty-two, with blond hair and a body to die for. She was always well-dressed and wore a lot of elaborately coordinated outfits. I wondered what she could possibly see in Curt, other than their shared race horse, "Dancer's Beauty." That horse was a champion pacer sulky stallion that won a lot of money for both of them at the Aurora Downs.

Sally wasn't around the YAK much, but when she was there, she collected the admission money at the door, particularly when the big name bands were playing. I also remember that she made several trips to Las Vegas with her sister-in-law, Beverly Hansen. She was always nice to me and very classy. They were certainly an odd couple, and it was obvious she was not into Curt for his looks or winning personality so the only thing left was his money, at least that was the only thing I could think of!

A lot of other people came out to see Curt, and he had a lot of associates. They typically paid him visits on weeknights when concerts were not taking place. I didn't know many of them, but I did see one guy who made frequent appearances. He was a short, balding man who tried to use a hat to try and cover up his receding hairline, and he had a few missing teeth. I met him once in the parking lot as he told me he was there to see his brother.

He introduced himself to me as Kenny and made small talk, asking me a lot of questions before he went in to play gin rummy with Curt. Little did I know that this shorter, slimmer man was often there to participate in talks about the ways to murder and dispose of George Jayne, a refined horseman from Park Ridge, on the North Side, who owned Happy Days Stables and was considered a bitter rival by his own brother, Silas Jayne.

One day in the early afternoon, Kenny showed up and asked me to drive him home to his stables. Someone had dropped him off there, and he had only been at the YAK for around twenty minutes so it all seemed a bit odd—almost orchestrated, to me.

I drove him back to his place, and we had the windows down in my car because it was a nice and warm summer day. He asked me many questions and had a strange twinkle in his eye as he pointed out the landmarks all along the way to his properties. I was not familiar with the area at all, but I was curious as he carefully worded his directions.

He kept on telling me, "You go this way here to get to my place, now don't forget!" as I drove him to 17201 South Central, Tinley Park, Illinois, directly attached to the Cook County Forest Preserves.

Sky Hi Stables 1969

At the back of Kenny's long dirt driveway, I could see a very large building with "Sky Hi Stables" written on it, in bold red letters. I drove to the end of the dirt road and into a gravel parking lot near a blue mobile home, to the right of the barn. I parked in front of it, as instructed by Kenny. He asked me if I wanted him to show me his place, and he also asked me if I liked horses.

As he opened the door of my car to get out, we were instantly surrounded by twenty to thirty Doberman Pinschers, barking and running around my car. I was afraid of all the dogs! Curt had one like them but dealing with this pack was nothing like facing a lone dog. I was quite overwhelmed. Kenny kept laughing at my fear of his dogs, telling me they wouldn't hurt me unless he put them up to it. After a while I got out of my car. Ken stood next to me, and, sure enough, there were no issues with the Dobes.

Kenny took me on a tour of his stables, starting at the south barn where he kept his show horses in twelve by twelve-foot box stalls with a cement isle. He showed me the club room, a ten-foot-wide fireplace with a flagstone mantle, a kitchen, washrooms with a shower, and several other rooms where saddles and other fine leather bridles were kept. There were three or four rooms with beds in them for stable hands that also featured an office. From this room you could see a fifty by one-hundred-foot indoor riding arena with large, Plexiglass windows and wooden bleachers for people to use while watching the horse shows from inside the clubroom. He next directed me to an area in the north barn with a few box stalls in front, stand stalls at the back, and a feed room for easy access.

As we walked to the back of that area, he opened the sliding door to show me a large mound of dirt that ran across the entire back of the building. The mound was about ten feet high, and I later learned that it was used as a backdrop for target practice. I was impressed through the tour of his facilities. He really had a fine place with some great design details, and I could tell he had put a lot of thought into its layout.

Now used to the many dogs that were running around us, I returned to my car. Kenny bid me goodbye, asking me if I knew my way back and telling me to come back whenever I wanted to. I headed back to Curt's place, thinking I would never return to Kenny's stables. Since Curt was not around, I just did a few things that needing doing and then finished some chores before calling it a day and going to bed.

CURTIS HANSEN'S
MODUS OPERANDI

I am compelled to mention again that Curt was up late at night, all of the time, as a side effect of his habitual use of weight-loss drugs. I thought he never slept as he and his brother played cards until about 3:00 a.m. at least two times a week. He frequently engaged his visitors until the very early daytime hours.

One particular morning as I woke up and dressed for the day, I began to look for him. It was about 11:00 a.m., and he was nowhere to be found. In his absence, I looked for things to do and was fixing a few things as I talked to his other hired help about the projects we were each working on and some other inconsequential matters.

It was a Friday, and later that night, as the featured band for that week was playing the YAK, Curt showed up and walked over to me, dressed in a flashy suit, clean shaven, with his hair combed, and a nice tie—a real rarity for him. He told me I needed to talk to him right after the show was done. His behavior seemed a bit odd to me, but he was my boss, so I nodded back to him as he went on his way.

I saw where Curt was headed and eventually followed him into another building. I witnessed him beating someone that I had never seen before. He was using a blackjack in one hand and a snub nose .38 revolver in his other. I kept my distance in the dark of that night, and he never saw me as I watched him mercilessly beat the man half to death. The guy was screaming in pain, but Curt didn't seem to pay any attention to his pleas. I made my way back to the main buildings with a knot in my stomach.

The band finished their show, packed up and left, and it was all quiet at the YAK since all of the patrons had left for the night. It was now time for me to go and see Curt. I was thinking about what my Uncle Roy had told me about Curt being a dangerous man as I went over to his work table near the kitchen.

He sat there attending to business matters and told me, "Billy, I don't need anyone around here like my worthless brother, that sleeps in until noon." I left the kitchen as Curt continued his business and wandered around the complex talking to various employees and informing them I was no longer employed and to see if they knew of other work, close by. It was now 1:00 a.m., and I saw Curt again. He had a smile on face as he said, "What you haven't left yet? Go get your stuff and GET!" I was in shock as I went to my room and packed my belongings and loaded them into the trunk of my car, not knowing where I'd go for the night.

I returned inside to ask him for some money, as he still needed to pay me for the last two weeks of work. He told me I never was worth the money he paid me and that it was time for me to go. I reflected on the events of the evening and thought it best to just keep my mouth shut and do precisely as I was told.

A Dark Night Gets Even Darker

There I was, out in the middle of nowhere, in the dead of night, far from my parents who always went to bed at 10:00 p.m. every night. As I drove out onto U.S. 30, I looked at my gas gauge and acknowledged that it was almost empty. I needed to get back to the city, and there certainly wasn't enough gas to get me there!

I drove on thinking of what Curt's brother Kenny had told me about how to find my way to the Sky Hi Stables and decided that was where I would head since it was the closest place I could think of. I continued my drive and adjusted the .45 caliber pistol that was holstered in the small of my back, finding my way to the driveway where Kenny lived with his wife, Beverly, and their two sons, Danny, a twelve-year-old and Mark, who was ten. I didn't want to disturb any of them, but I needed a place to stay and was out of better options. I was desperate, and Kenny had, after all, invited me to return to his place any time. Circumstances had led me to take him at his word.

When I got to the driveway, I saw a dim light way back off the road that was coming from the house trailer. I drove all the way down the driveway and parked my car in front of it. The dogs were barking and all over the place as Kenny came to the door with a .25 caliber pistol in his hand. When he saw it was me, he calmed down the dogs. It seemed as if he was expecting me.

Kenny stood on the porch and turned the outside light on as he smiled and told me it was okay and that the dogs wouldn't hurt me, saying, "Come on in!" I went in, and he asked me if I wanted a cup of coffee, telling me it was bad well water but he boiled it. That didn't sound too appealing to me so I asked him if he had a soda or something else. He reached up in the kitchen cabinet and pulled out an unopened bottle of Cutty Sark Scotch and two clean glasses, telling me this is all he had and that he was a Scotch drinker.

I told him I was hungry, and I sat there as he made me a pair of bologna sandwiches. I was eying the two glasses on the kitchen table, filled halfway with the scotch. He told me he was surprised to see me as I began eating a sandwich. I told him my tale of woe while I ate and drank what he had offered me. I remember the sensation as the scotch burned my throat each time I took a drink.

Kenny asked me if I knew anything about organized crime and explained that his brother was a hitman for the mafia but it was called "The Outfit" here in Chicago. I told him I had seen Curt beat a man with a blackjack that previous night, and Ken advised me to never talk about it to anyone. We spoke about a lot of things that night. He asked about my service in the Marine Corps, and what they taught me. I simply told him, "They taught me a lot, mostly discipline."

He said, "They teach you to kill, huh? That's what they taught my brother!" He obviously knew the answer to that question but couldn't help but hear a confirmatory response from me.

At one point he asked me if I had ever heard of "The Peterson Murders." When I told him I didn't know anything about them, he told me it was a very famous case and had made headlines in the newspapers a few years ago. We were both getting really drunk as he continued. He told me that he had almost made headlines himself because he had done it. He also told me that his brother helped him clean up the mess and dump the bodies. He claimed that it had all happened at the Idle Hour Stables.

It was clear to me that Kenny was trying very hard to impress me. He spoke of many things late into the night, and we drank the bottle dry. He then offered me some marijuana, and I just put up my hand and told him that I didn't use drugs.

I was entirely drunk and very dizzy by now as he took my car keys and put them on top of the corner kitchen cabinet, telling me, with a twinkle in his eye, "I think you're too drunk to drive so you can stay here for the night." He said that his wife and kids were somewhere else, so everything would be fine.

Kenny led me past a bedroom of Doberman puppies to a second bedroom with bunk beds and told me I could sleep there, in the kids' room. After the lights were off and I had undressed down to my skivvies, I climbed into the bottom bunk, hiding my .45 under the pillow, as was my custom. I started to fall asleep. It had been a long and difficult day for me.

I soon woke up with a start to find Kenneth Hansen touching my genitals and, in a quiet voice, asking me, "Do you want me to kiss it for you?"

I instantly lifted myself forward and put my hand in his chest, authoritatively cautioning him, "Do you know what you're doing? Just back off!"

He replied, "I'm not going to hurt you." With that, he silently slunk away into the master bedroom. To me, he was a drunk and dirty old man who was obviously queer.

I laid back in bed and slept for a while longer. As the sun rose, Kenny came into the room, and I reached back under my pillow to feel for my .45. It was still there. He told me to get dressed and get out of the trailer, using the back door. I did just that.

I was still tired, hungover, and hungry with no gas in my car—or even its keys! I walked out by the barn and saw his barn hands feeding the horses and a blond-haired guy about my age, well built and bare-chested. His distinctive suntan bespoke the fact that he frequently went without a shirt. He was loading shavings into the shavings wagon. The wagon was used to transport fresh wood shavings into the stalls after they were cleaned and ready for new bedding. He saw me coming out of the back door, and he looked upset that I had just left it. He came over to me, asking me what I was doing in the trailer. His southern drawl and poor grammar usage made him seem like a real hillbilly.

I asked him who he was, and he told me his name was Roger. He looked rather angry with me. He asked me if Kenny had told me about the Peterson boys. I told him, "He's all yours. I'm not into that."

His voice was now angry, and his fists were tightly clenched as he retorted, "Are you calling me queer?"

I reached my hand behind my back to check my pistol and said, "No, and I'm not looking for trouble, Roger," as I stood ready for it.

Roger went into the trailer, and I spent the next few hours getting acquainted with the other hands who worked at the stables. Kenny finally emerged at about 2:00 p.m. Roger was not with him. I got the impression that he and Kenny were closer than what I had initially thought. Kenny came out with my car keys in hand and a sandwich as he put a coin in a soft drink machine he had on site and bought me a Coke.

I told him I didn't have any gas in my car, and he put some in from a five-gallon gas can and gave me $20.00, telling me, "You can repay me after I get your money from my brother, if you come back."

He also told me that "we" didn't like to be called "queer" and that "we" preferred the term "gay." This clarified a few impressions that I had of Kenny and Roger's relationship.

He gave me his business card with a phone number on the back and informed me that it was the number to a nightclub where I might find a job.

These Hansen brothers were certainly strange, unusual people to me and were far different than anyone I had ever known! I thanked him and left to the city where I found the owner of the establishment he referred me to on Rush Street. I went in, and sure enough, I landed a job as a barkeep.

Outfit Bars and Adult Book Store

T ime passed rather quickly for me as I worked for a B-Girl/Stripper Club that traded bartenders back and forth with other needy establishments. If one guy didn't show up for work, then someone had to fill his place for the night—or however long the owner wanted you to work. The name of the owner of the place was Nicki Stevens, AKA Nicholas Stevenopalos, and the name of his bar was Inferno's. There was another bar below his that was housed in the basement. It was aptly called The Snake Pit and was owned and managed by Vito Dominicus.

Across the street from us was The Crystal Pistol, owned by Marvin Moline, and down the street from there, on the corner of Burton and Wells, was the Nocturne: the longest running B-Girl Bar in the city of Chicago, owned by Bill Niff.

The Nocturne was a private club and had been around since 1938. It had such influence and political connections that its loyal patrons were members for decades, many of whom were now well past retirement age. It was at Inferno's where I first met a rather dapperly dressed fellow named Louie "The Mooch" Eboli. Louie paid routine visits to each of these Outfit-owned establishments to make sure they weren't being cheated out of any street tax.

Other than the occasional visit of mob guys, we also saw different FBI agents make the rounds at the bars while the owners were away. The agents really stood out in the way they dressed and carried themselves. They were also always found in pairs, wore white shirts and ties, and full suits with wing-tip shoes. They were clean cut with short haircuts, almost military looking in their appearance and bearing. They would never take a seat, but they would approach the bartender and ask to talk for a minute.

They asked if they knew certain organized crime figures and would ask about other organized crime activities—or if they knew police who were on the take from the Mob.

They always got a standard answer of, "I can't help you. I don't know anything about it." We were schooled, by the bar owners, to ask them if they wanted a drink and to be polite with them but never give up any information. I always avoided contact with them and let another bartender address them.

On one of the visits of the FBI agents that I observed, I saw the agent pull out a business card and hand it to the barkeep. The bartender held onto it until the agents left and then tossed it into the trash. Later on in that shift, I tactfully made my way to the garbage receptacle and retrieved the business card. I was curious what it was and what was written on it. I concealed it in my front shirt pocket and later put it into my wallet, after I got off of work and made it somewhere safe.

It was a very basic, simple card that had bold black type with 'FBI' in the center and the agent's name and phone number on the lower left hand corner and a blank back. No address was present, and it was as no nonsense a business card as I had ever seen and stood out for its sheer blandness.

One day Vito was filling in for someone at the Over 21 Book Store, down the street. It was an adult-themed bookstore with booths in the back that played different porn films in each of its chambers. He asked me if I knew anything about air-conditioning since the one there wasn't working.

I told him, "Sure I know a little about it, just let me take a look at it." I went down the street to see if I could get it working and it was a basic problem so I was able to fix it.

Sometime later on, I asked for a job at the store, and they hired me. This place made more money than all the bars put together! It was a 24-hour operation that never closed. They put me on the night shift with my dog, a large Doberman, that would scare anyone who tried to even touch the counter, much less try to hurt me, as they were frequently a target of project street thugs from neighboring Cabrini Green.

It was midnight to 8:00 a.m. for a while, and I was up for the change of duties that it offered and hopes for better pay. Particularly appealing to me was the fact that I didn't have to suggest, "Buy the lady a drink, sir?"

One night Bill Niff asked me to come over to the Nocturne to tend bar for him, filling an earlier shift. I wanted the money so I told him I could do it for him, but I still had to report to work at the Over 21 by midnight. Bill agreed that would be fine so I went to work for him in the late afternoon.

After I got behind the bar to begin the shift at the Nocturne, I noticed Curtis Hansen sitting at a table, all alone. He waved at me with a smiling face, and Bill told me to go over and greet him. He asked me to sit down at his table where he pulled out a tattered membership card and said, proudly displaying the date on his card, "I bet ya never knew that I've been a member here this long!"

We talked about how I got there and what I had been doing since I left the YAK. He acted like his discharge of me was nothing to be concerned about, even after I told him about how his brother tried to molest me. That was the first of the many times I heard him say, "I wanted a brother, but I wound up with two sisters!" He laughed at his joke while describing his perception of Kenny. He also confided to me that Kenny was the brains behind a lot of different ventures, including the Valley View YAK, and he said, "We were supposed to be partners, but he had nothing to offer the business!"

He further expressed his reservations in Kenny's ability to keep his hands off of the many young men who would frequent the YAK as customers. We talked about my employment, and he was very curious about the amount of money that I told him the "porn shop down the street" raked in each night.

Curtis had torched the YAK Club in an effort to collect on the insurance policy money. It was a terrible idea that resulted in a total loss for him because he forgot to pay his insurance premium! He had lost all of his World War II souvenirs—which included two genuine samurai swords he took from his tour in Japan—along with his Cadillacs, other vehicles, furniture, buildings, and everything else he owned.

He watched the place burn to the ground as the Frankfurt Fire Department refused to put the fire out and just sat there, watching it burn with him and several neighbors and onlookers who happened to stop by for the show.

One firefighter told him and the other bystanders, "You're beyond the city limits, and we don't have to put it out!" as he referred to the blaze.

They were obviously resentful that he had kept the club private and refused their suggestions to work with their city to make that amazing pool a shared, public attraction, and they weren't about to step in to help him in his time of need.

Curt was now working for Irwin Weiner, operating and selling mobile hot dog stands. Irv had been running a scam on welfare clinics and other businesses from the scim that came from the Teamster's Pension Fund loan that the Outfit used to finance Circus Circus in Las Vegas. Other ventures were also involved, such as a fiberglass factory in Bensenville, a southwest suburb of Chicago, Illinois, owned and operated by Danny Seifert. The different businesses were used to funnel money to Joey Lombardo, Irv Weiner, and "Milwaukee Phil" [Felix Alderisio].

In response to Curt's question on how I had made out since we had last spoken, I told him that I was doing well and was making a good living. I followed his lead, and we didn't discuss my time with him back at the YAK.

"That's fine for you. I'm not doing so well, and neither is my brother."

Curt's lack of mortgage payments had also resulted in his loss of his many apartment buildings in Chicago Heights. Kenny's wife, Beverly, had filed for divorce, and they were now separated. Curt's wife, Sally, had left him and went out to Arizona for another man.

I can't say that I blamed either of them now that I knew more about these brothers and their many perversions. Beverly had even procured compromising photos of her homosexual husband in bed with their barn manager, as she took photos of the scene herself after returning home from a jaunt to Las Vegas. She had used the threat of the photos, in courtroom proceedings, to procure anything she wanted from Kenny. He was intimidated into submission to any and all of her demands while they worked out their affairs.

Curt drilled me on the earnings that were coming in at my other job at the Over 21 and was extremely interested as I laid things out to him. He asked me, "How would you like to own your own place?"

I was interested, to say the least. He asked me to help his brother keep tabs on his stables and keep them profitable because his wife had taken control of it by court order.

He told me, "Man with no money in pocket roars like mouse. Man with money in pocket roars like lion." Curt left the bar, telling me he needed to get the okay [from an Outfit boss] to open shop before we could proceed and also told me, "If you help me out, then I'll help you out. Who knows? We may get rich off of this!"

The next day I went to Nicki Steven's to get the money that he owed me. He told me to get lost and that he was never going to pay me. The district manager of the Over 21 told me I could never become a manager much less own my own place, while he brandished a pistol at me.

It was apparent that I wasn't going to get where I wanted by working with them so I took Curt up on his offer. I drove out to the Sky Hi Stables to ask Beverly Hansen for a job. I arrived in the nick of time to help keep her from losing the place, as she was two months behind on her mortgage payments and in desperate need of my management skills.

OFF TO HELP THE
HANSEN BROTHERS

C urt told me to call his brother, Kenny, who was then living in an apartment that was rented by Ralph Capone's nephew in Oak Forest. Ralph's nephew was a bookie for the Outfit during the daytime and allowed Kenny to stay at the place at night with Kenny's companion, Roger Spry. Kenny stayed in the place because it was close to his former stables that were now in Beverly's possession, as they were legally separated.

I made the call and Kenny asked me to meet him at the Greek restaurant across the street from his apartment on 159th Street in Oak Forest, about four miles away from Sky Hi Stables. I drove out to meet him, and we had breakfast together. Kenny and I talked about how well I was doing and that with the help of himself and Curt, I could open my own business.

Before we could proceed with our plans Kenny needed my help driving him around to procure a driver's license, as he had lost it several years ago and had never tried to recover it, and a car. That way he could start another business venture for himself in order to make a living and keep up on his child support payments.

I was living in the bunkhouse of the Sky Hi at that time and was helping his wife, Beverly, out with the day-to-day business operations that she had taken over after their legal separation. That placed me in a position that Kenny wanted to exploit for a number of reasons. I did need his help to get things going for my own business so I was basically at his beck and call for a few months while we worked on things.

One day while Kenny was off taking care of some personal matters, I went out with Curt in his red Gremlin to do some business of our own. We went to see Jimmy "The Bomber" Catuara at his home in Oak Lawn. It was a lavish home. I remember Curtis and I had to wait in the foyer, and Curt looked up at an ornate chandelier and chuckled, "Who says crime doesn't pay!"

Jimmy came down from the upstairs, and Curt introduced him to me. Jimmy spoke broken English with a thick Italian accent. He was a slight man around 5' 5" tall, and he was dressed in cashmere trousers, a nice sport shirt, and particularly fancy shoes.

In New York he would have been referred to as a "Don" and the head of his own family, but in Chicago he was simply termed a "Made Guy." I later learned that he had taken the Oath of Omerta back in the 1940s. I was impressed because Jimmy was the first "Made Guy" in the Outfit that I had ever personally met.

* * *

Jimmy told Curt that we had the okay to put slot machines in designated taverns in Chicago Heights, which was Al Pilotto's, another Made Guy's territory. Pilotto's brother was the Chief of Police there. We now had a job to do so we got to it.

The following day Curt and I loaded up a trailer with slot machines. They had been stored in Bally's warehouse, located on Saginaw Street on the North Side of Chicago. We took them to various taverns and introduced them to their new homes. All of the places we visited were connected with the Outfit either by direct line of ownership or a subterfuge liquor license with a hidden owner.

We had no problems from any of the owners as we set up the machines. We pushed ourselves to get as many installed as possible before nightfall and then did the same thing the next day. The slots were in place, and now all that we had to do was empty the money from the machines and bring it back to Jimmy. This was how Curt and I gathered some of the funding to get our business venture started.

Most of these places were strategically located close to the steel mills and foundries where workers could cash their paychecks at the tavern and then spend their hard-earned money on some in-house drinking and gambling. The slot machines were perfectly positioned to cash in on the locals—and we literally had our hands full as we cleaned them out each day.

A few weeks later Jimmy called us in again and told us that Al Pilotto was furious and wanted all of the machines removed. We went back around and uninstalled every last one of them. They had been bringing in hundreds of thousands of dollars to Jimmy, but he never gave a cut to Pilotto, so the slots had to go.

With nothing to do now, we talked to Jimmy about opening up a porn shop/adult bookstore. We needed his blessing, and that of his associates, but it was also going to take some time to get everything in place from our side. Curt went back to Weenie World and his hot dog stands. I went back to Sky Hi Stables, driving Kenny around to places such as Silas Jayne's Stables in Elgin, IL.

Around this time, I learned that Irv Weiner, "Milwaukee Phil" Alderisio, Joey Lombardo, Tony Spilotro, Curt, and another man named Danny Seifert were all laundering money from the teamster's loan that was given to Circus Circus in Las Vegas. They had skimmed money from the loan itself, not putting it into Circus Circus but directly into their own pockets.

It was public knowledge that Allen Glick and the owners of Argent Enterprises had secured their loan from the Teamsters Union. What was not publicly known was the fact that a "service fee" for making the arrangements to obtain the loan had been received by the Chicago Outfit through Jimmy Hoffa or Allen Dorfman, who at the time of the loan was serving as the President of the Teamster's Pension Fund. Something to note is that Jimmy Hoffa, while he served as President of the Pension Fund, had his office in Washington D.C. while Dorfman had an office in Chicago.

Allen Dorfman Mugshot

This was a pretty typical Outfit arrangement where a business was used as a front to show goods and services were being provided and exchanged, but the margins of profit for the services rendered were often too good to be true. This fact, historically, has been used by the Feds to their advantage in many court proceedings where they have prosecuted criminal operations for income tax evasion rather than their violent crimes that could not be substantiated and proved by trial. The IRS and its auditors have frequently teamed with the FBI for operations of this nature.

* * *

About a month after we removed the slot machines, Jimmy called Curt and told us to meet him at his home. We arrived there, and Jimmy said, "Go see Joey [Lombardo], he's a good boy. He'll take care of you." After giving us his blessing for our business, Jimmy also told me to go out to Las Vegas and bring him back a pair of shoes, shoes unlike any of the hundreds of other ones that he already owned.

I now knew he trusted me. He told me to drive my car and stay at the Stardust Hotel where all my expenses would be paid, except for the shoes, of course. This was a great chance for me to shine, and there was no way I was going to blow this new opportunity.

First Time in Sin City

I was off to Las Vegas! It took a very long two-day drive before I finally checked in at the Stardust Hotel. After I parked my car, I took my suitcase to the front counter to discuss my arrangements with the staff. The desk clerk called the manager after I gave him my name and said, "Yes, your room has been reserved—anything you need, just sign for it."

Let me explain a few things about the Stardust, as it was unique for its time. There were a lot of rooms at the Stardust, and they had a number of innovations that were very user-friendly for their gambling business. The main building had an elevator and some of the nicest suites in all of Vegas. They had satellite rooms that were named after the planets of our solar system, from Mercury to Pluto. The satellite units were separate from the main building and were cheaper, more like a basic motel than the full service hotel suites housed in the Stardust itself.

It was said that Tony Accardo came up with the idea so middle income people would be able to stay there for a lot less than the other hotel casinos, and he was right. They flocked in from everywhere. The Stardust was the "Flagship" of the hotels in Las Vegas and the Chicago Outfit owned it.

The bellhop carried my suitcase to my room, opened the door, and handed me the key as I tipped him. My suite was fabulous! It had a living room with nice overstuffed furniture, a dining room, comfortable bedroom and bathroom with televisions in the living room and bedroom. The place was very nice, but I didn't come there to stay in for the weekend.

I went downstairs and ate some dinner and was off to the blackjack table. I bought ten dollars' worth of chips and lost my first hand. In the second hand, I doubled down and won. I was tired from my drive, but the excitement of the place kept me playing cards until about 4:00 a.m. I was ahead about three thousand dollars as I cashed in my chips in what I thought would be the end of my night. I went back up to my room and got into bed. Two hours later, I awoke feeling like I had just had eight hours of sleep. I showered, changed, and got dressed back into my suit.

I was off to the casino again, only this time I was playing blackjack with five dollar chips. Every time I would win a hand the dealer would pay me with larger value chips than what I had put down in an attempt to make me bet the higher value chips, which I did.

After sixteen hours at the table and several dealer changes, I had stacks and stacks of chips in front of me.

I had been so engaged in playing that it took a while before I noticed that they were black in color—indicating that they were the Stardust's $100.00 chips. I was betting two or three at a time when it dawned on me that I was betting more than three months' rent on the turn of a card! Reality hit me pretty hard at that point so I then decided to stop and count my winnings. I had a little over forty thousand dollars in chips, and there was a crowd around my table, playing and watching me win.

I stretched back, lit a cigarette, and said, "I could use a drink."

The dealer called over a cocktail waitress that asked me what I wanted to drink. I said, "Royal Salute, straight up with a water back." She returned, and I went to pay for it, but she told me it was on the house.

As I put the glass of scotch to my lips, it tasted more like a well scotch than top-shelf, and I told her so. She insisted that it was Royal Salute, and I said, "Never mind, keep it." I started gathering my chips.

Suddenly, a man came up to her with a fresh, unopened fifth of Royal Salute. She opened it and poured me a drink in a new glass, leaving me the bottle and a pitcher of water along with a glass full of ice. I gulped some down and followed it with the cool water. That was the stuff!

I played several more hands of blackjack and began losing. I thought it was a good time to cash in my chips and quit. As I left the table, somebody immediately took my seat.

A lady carried my chips for me as I cashed them in. The cashier asked me if I wanted a check or cash. I told her, "Cash." She counted out the hundred dollar bills very briskly, just like a bank-teller. As she counted the money aloud, I realized that there was still over thirty thousand dollars in total winnings, as my take.

I took my money in a hotel-marked envelope and went to eat my breakfast. I had four eggs, bacon, toast, a glass of milk, and some orange juice. As I looked at my wristwatch, I was shocked to see that it was now 3:30 in the afternoon. The fact that there were no clocks in the casino had impacted my perception of time. I went to my room, showered, and hit the sack.

I fell into a deep sleep and woke up, again feeling very refreshed. I looked at my watch again, and it was about five in the afternoon of the following day. I had slept for over twenty-four hours, and I thought it was a good time to shop for the pair of shoes for Jimmy.

I went down to the haberdashery and saw a pair of white, patent-leather shoes with genuine silver buckles that really caught my eye. I asked the clerk if they had them in Jimmy's size and he brought me back a shoebox with them in it.

I paid for the shoes and gulped when the clerk said, "That'll be $125.00. Cash or charge, sir?"

"Cash." I then paid for the shoes and took them back with me to my room.

Little did I know that years later I would see on the news that Jimmy Catuara was murdered on Hubbard Street and Ogden Avenue wearing the very same shoes I had bought for him. It was many years later, but I saw it shown on TV as his legs dangled out of his Cadillac as he tried to escape it and was gunned down.

Having settled that item of business, it was off to the gaming tables again! I started playing blackjack. This time I gave the dealer $500.00, and he asked me how I wanted my chips. I told him I wanted $5, $10, $20 and $50 chips, and they were very accommodating. I started betting with the $10 chips. I kept losing, so I doubled my bets. After buying more and continuing to lose, I knew that it was time to quit. The thought kept going through my mind that these little wooden-feeling disks were real money.

I asked for a rack to carry my chips to the cashier. I cashed them in and now had a little over $25,000 left of my total winnings, after taxes had been deducted. I was hungry again and went in to the restaurant and ordered a good steak dinner with a baked potato, salad, and the whole nine yards.

I Become the Transporter

As I was eating my food, a man in his mid-forties came over and sat next to me in my booth

"You must be Red."

As we shook hands, I asked him who he was. He told me, "We have a mutual friend. You know, the guy with the shoes that sent you out here."

He then asked me how I had done at the tables, and I answered, "Better than I thought I would! This is my first time in Las Vegas." The man smiled and told me he had something for me to take back to Jimmy when I was ready to leave.

I told him that I would be leaving in the morning, and he told me, "When you check out, the desk clerk will give you something. Make sure you keep it in your trunk and don't drive too fast."

As he got up to leave he told me, "Be safe now, ya hear?"

"I understand."

Moments later, with my stomach gorged with good food, I felt sleepy and went back to my room and went to bed.

The following morning, I packed my suitcase and headed for the front desk to check out. I signed the check-out slip that the clerk gave me, without giving him any money, and he gave me a locked duffle bag. It was made of a supple brown leather and had a tiny lock that was fixed to a d-ring at the end. It was about a foot long by eight inches wide and no more than a foot in height, with a pair of fine leather handles. Although I had a good idea of what was in it, I never felt around it to investigate.

Along with my own suitcase, I put Jimmy's in the trunk of my car and made a left hand turn onto the Strip. Looking down at my gas gage, I only had a quarter tank left so I stopped at a gas station to fill up. I couldn't help but notice that even the gas stations had slot machines. Slot machines were everywhere. I paid for my gas, got back into my car, and told myself "I am not going to stop one more time until I am out of Nevada!" I could tell that I still had a severe case of gambling fever and needed to get out of that place.

I breathed a huge sigh of relief as I crossed the state line, and I drove on to the south rim of the Grand Canyon where I checked into a motel, as the sun began to set. I left the motel and headed for a restaurant for yet another steak dinner. With a thousand dollars in my pocket and the rest of my winnings safely tucked away in my suitcase, I said to myself, "No more cheeseburgers for me!"

After feeling full, I went back to my motel room and got a good night's sleep. I awoke early the next morning to the sound of braying mules. I looked out the window and saw a dozen or so in a wooden corral that were frolicking together and kind of noisy. I got dressed and walked outside, breathing in the clean, fresh air. The motel was a sort of log cabin with nice rooms.

As I walked down the stairs of the porch, reading the directional signs for all of the tourists, I reached the end of the parking lot where several trailheads began. I took a brief walk down a winding trail that had warning signs that were made with bark-covered branches that said things like "Mule rescue is expensive!" I walked down for an hour or so, passing many other cautionary signs, and then turned around and went back up the trail to get some breakfast.

After eating a hearty breakfast, I checked out of the motel and I was back onto the road to Chicago. I only stopped for food and gas until I reached Joliet, Illinois. Now I was close to home.

I drove to my apartment on the North Side and unloaded the two bags from the trunk and went inside. I put the bags up and crashed on my bed, sleeping until around noon the next day. I had made it home, safe and sound.

THE DROP OFF AND FALLOUT

When I woke up, I had breakfast and called Curt Hansen. He told me to pick him up about four doors down from Marion's place at Claremont and Foster, right by the firehouse.

I went and picked him up, and we drove to Jimmy's place in Oak Lawn, stopping for a cheeseburger. When we got to Jimmy's, Curt asked me to give him the bag that I had brought with me. I opened the trunk and gave him the bag, and we went and rang the doorbell.

Jimmy personally answered the door with a smile on his face as Curt handed him the bag. I said, "Wait a minute!" as I went back to the car and returned with the shoebox which I then handed to Jimmy.

His face lit up with an even bigger smile as he said, in his thick Italian accent, "You remember me!"

We all went in the house to a covered screen porch at the back. As we sat down, he opened the shoebox and in a joyful voice he said, "Whatta fina pair a shoes, I donna gotta pair a shoes this nice! Thank you!" and I smiled at him as he smiled at me. The two of them talked and then we left. Jimmy said goodbye to both of us, and we drove straight to American Bonding.

I drove the car into the parking lot, and we went in together. Joey wasn't there, but Irv Weiner was, along with several other people. Irv began to speak to me about my former employers. He asked me how long they had owed me money and I answered, "Several months, now."

"Come on. Where's your car?"

He and I climbed into my car, leaving Curt behind at American Bonding. I didn't know what was going to happen next, but I was sure things were going to get interesting for my former bosses!

Irvin Weiner MugShot

Irv and I drove to the Inferno first. We walked in, and Irv looked at Nicki Stevens and said, "When are you going pay this kid what you owe him?" Nick walked with Irv into his back office.

When they came out, Nick handed me a check. I told Nick, "You never paid me with a check before, and I want cash now."

Nick started to say something, and Irv cut him off, saying, "I told you to make that kid happy, now make him happy! Give him his cash." Nick reached under the bar and gave me the money that he owed me.

Irv said, "Give us a drink."

Nick, in a humble voice, said, "What are you guys having?"

Irv ordered a 7/7 and I had club soda. Irv never paid for the drinks, and we got up and left.

As we got in my car to leave, I asked Irv what he told Nick, and he said that I didn't need to know. He then told me, "Let's get on to the other place down the street."

I cautioned Irv, warning him that the guy at the Over 21 kept a .45 underneath the counter. Irv told me, "They didn't stop making guns when he bought his!" as he showed me the small .38 snub nose in his left suit-jacket pocket.

We went in to the Over 21 Book Store, and Dan Jehoviac, the manager, was there.

Irv told him, "Give the kid his money."

We stood there waiting for his reaction.

Dan looked us over and then said, "I'm not giving him a damn thing!" as he reached for his pistol.

Irv reached over in his pocket and gripped the .38 at his side and slapped Dan with his right hand. He ordered Dan to get down from the raised counter and go into the office.

Dan tried to lock the door once he was inside, and Irv pushed the door in with his shoulder, pointing his pistol at Dan's face. Irv told him, in a raging voice, "When are you guys going to learn? Give the kid his money!"

A flustered, red-faced Dan held out a hand full of cash and said, "Take it!"

Irv looked over at me and said, "Go ahead and take it all."

It was much more than he owed me, but I did what I was told.

As we walked out of the place, Irv looked up and down the street as he put his index finger in my chest and said, "Find some kind of store, as close to this one as you can get, and rent it."

We climbed into my car and drove back to American Bonding as I counted the money. There was more than a thousand dollars, and I told Irv, "This is more than what they owe me."

He replied, "That's okay, kid, you're going to put them out of business." He smiled while he looked ahead.

I now noticed that his monogrammed, custom glasses had his initials etched into the top corner of the lens. I had never seen anything quite so flashy before in my life!

I drove Irv back to American Bonding, and Curt had already left so I went back to my apartment, musing about the events of the day. The Outfit had a very different approach to handling business than anything I had ever experienced.

My First Real Estate and Another Venture

The apartment building I called home was located on Carmen Street about eight buildings west of Broadway. It was a six flat, constructed of brick with a new boiler that heated each of the units. The apartments had mahogany crown moldings and baseboards with a wall safe in the walk-in closet which really made them stand out as nice places to live. Each apartment was identical: a three bedroom, two-bathroom unit with washing facilities for each tenant along with storage, a boiler room, and a workshop. The whole building and grounds were in very good shape and had been well maintained for a number of years.

The building was for sale so I knocked on my landlord's door and told him that I wanted to buy it. After we negotiated a price, he agreed to owner finance it. Several weeks later, I had full ownership of it and raised all of my tenants' rent and moved in to the former landlord's apartment, keeping one of the four available garages for myself. This upset several of the four remaining tenants. Some of them moved out, but I quickly found replacements for them.

In under a month I had the place filled again by just putting a sign up in the window. I felt very self-satisfied on the purchase and looked forward to other profitable ventures to come my way.

Around this same time, I began open communications with federal authorities to help clean things up in my area. I made an effort to contact the FBI. After Special Agent John Osborne's fruitless efforts to get any bartenders to talk to him, I had picked up a business card with his name on it that I had retrieved from the trash can and stored in my wallet a few months earlier. He stood out to me because I recognized him from several visits to various locations, and I almost felt sorry for him.

I called the FBI from the number on the card and asked to speak to S/A John Osborne. I identified myself, at his request, and I explained to him that people were laughing at him. He was never going to get an employee to give him information and thus put himself out of work.

I told him I would give him all of the information he needed, but that it had to be on my terms. He agreed and wanted to meet with me. I laid things out and said I would meet with him at the Lion House in the Lincoln Park Zoo at about 1:30 p.m. the following day. He asked me how he would recognize me.

I explained, "You won't need to recognize me. I will recognize you." At that point, the conversation ended, and I hung up the phone.

THE FBI AND I MEET

In August of 1971, I met S/A John Osborne at about 1:00 p.m. at the Lincoln Park Zoo, inside the Lion House, as we had agreed. I was walking around in a work shirt and blue jeans with cowboy boots, surveying the area to see how many agents would show up. I saw a man looking at one of the big cats, eating popcorn, wearing a suit, white socks, and wing-tipped shoes that made him stand out like a sore thumb.

I casually walked over to him, also looking at the big cat, and said, "You must be John."

He immediately led me to the back door where another agent was waiting. They drove me to Evanston, Illinois, a northern suburb of Chicago that had no mob influence, where it would be safe to talk. They led me into a restaurant for lunch where we discussed what I knew about the Outfit. John explained to me that providing them with information would never get me rich, but they would pay me for my expenses.

I was determined to set my own rules about giving them information on organized crime activities, and they would have to decide on whether or not to accept what I offered. I shared information with him regarding specific police officers on the take and the money they received.

I could tell from that first meeting with John that he would be easy for me to work with and that he would keep things confidential. He proposed calling all information into him, and him alone, using the name of my former Marine Corps company commander as a codename to confirm it was me, on his own private line so that I wouldn't have to go through the FBI switchboard.

John was curious why I contacted him, as he had been trying to talk to other bartenders that worked in Outfit joints and had never been able to get anyone to share information with him. I told him they had bullied and hurt people who were afraid of them, including me.

The people he had tried to interview simply wouldn't help him and he had a hard time coming to terms with it and couldn't see why they weren't stepping up to do the right thing. What he just couldn't understand was this simple economic fact: why would someone help him and risk getting murdered, or at the very least, be out of a good paying job, if their boss was indicted and the business closed as a result of their testimony to the Feds?

I had my own reasons for coming forward. I wanted to try to stop some of the police who took payoffs along with the people who paid them to look the other way while they lavished in crime. I really wanted to end the vicious murder cycle where thugs and hit men got away with anything they wanted because people refused to take a stand against them. These Outfit hitmen were literally getting away with murder—and I wanted to stop it.

I returned home and made plans on how I was going to proceed with my business and personal dealings. The stage was now set for some intensely informative maneuvering.

GROWING A BUSINESS

I went back to Old Town, looking for a storefront to rent for the bookstore. I couldn't find anything in that area except for an old building that was set back off of the street and was pretty run down. There was a hotdog stand that was owned by a Korean family that took up half of the lot, leaving a long, paved driveway that led back to the building of interest.

The building itself was built in 1897, and at the time of its construction, it served as a blacksmith shop with a carriage house that was made to accommodate both carriages and horses. It had barn doors that swung out, when opened. As I first looked at it, I could see piles of debris and junk from floor to the top of the fourteen-foot-high ceiling, not to mention all of the garbage housed upstairs on the second floor. It had taken a long time to acquire all of that stuff, and it would take a lot of effort just to clear it out. I can't say that the thought of it made me happy, but it was clearly the best option I had so I decided to go for it.

Sam Napaderno, an aged gentleman in his late seventies, owned the place and agreed on a five-year lease with a five-year option after I haggled with him about the price. Rent was to be $25.00 a month for the first year, and each following year an additional $25.00 per month would be tacked onto the monthly payment. He also allowed me six months' rent free to clean it up before making my first payment to him. It was a building lease, meaning I was responsible for the entire building, which included the hotdog stand in the front, although they still paid Sam separate monthly rent.

I drove to American Bonding looking for Curt. I found him there playing cards with one of the other bondsmen. I told him that I had found a place and had rented it. When I showed him the lease, he said, "Wow, what a deal! Let's go look at it."

I drove him there, pulled into the driveway, and we got out while I opened the barn doors.

"Well that explains the $25.00 a month rent with six months' rent free," he chuckled. "This place is gonna take a whole lot of cleanin' up. Kenny and you are gonna have your work cut out for ya. I'll get the money to build it."

I asked him where he was going to get the money, and he told me, "I'm going to borrow it from Francis Carnacle, from Whippany, New Jersey." whom Curt had known since his days in the Marine Corps.

I drove Curt back and bid him goodbye as I headed home, stopping for a steak dinner along the way. I didn't hear from Curt or Kenny for a few days, at which time, Curt asked me to meet him at the Country Corner Kitchen, a restaurant in Tinley Park. We sat down and ordered breakfast.

While we were waiting for our food, Curt pulled out a pen and began to write on a napkin. As he wrote on the napkin, he told me, "I'm putting up the money. My sister, Kenny, who is allergic to manual labor, isn't doing anything, and you are going to have to do all the work. I'll help you as much as possible."

He showed me the napkin where he had written all three of our names: Kenny, Curt and Billy, saying, "What do we need Kenny for? You think he is gonna go down there and work? We'll see the next Coming first!"

I watched him draw a line through Kenny's name, and then he said, "We are fifty-percent partners now instead of thirds."

I was quick to tell him, "We were all partners to start with. Why do you want to cut him out?"

At that remark, he told me, "If you wanna give him half of your half for doing nothing, go right ahead."

On another, separate napkin he drew up a written agreement for a partnership between him and me. He explained, "This is not a legal contract, it's just so you and I won't have any problems with our responsibilities in the future." We both initialed the napkin, and he put it into his pocket.

With our partnership now formally confirmed, we finished eating and left the restaurant. Curt went on his way, giving me some cash to use to begin fixing up the place.

I called a waste removal company and gave them the address to the building that I had just rented and requested some construction dumpsters be dropped off there ASAP. I then looked around for some help with the clearing out process. This was not a one-man job and removal of the junk from the scrap-heap was going to take some extra hands and backs—or there'd be no way to make the current dumping grounds into a useable space for a store.

I hired two "bust out kids" to help me with the dirty work. I don't know how many 30-yard dumpsters we filled that day, but as it began to get dark, we had three quarters of the first floor cleared and empty. That's when I noticed, with great disappointment, that there was a dirt floor beneath all of the debris!

The next day, the waste removal company hauled away the last dumpster-load of junk, and I paid the guys for their help and bought them both a hotdog from the hotdog stand out front. It was fitting because all of us had worked until we were dog tired.

I went home and showered, changed clothes, and went out to have a good meal. I called Curt and said, "Curt, you're not gonna believe this, but the joint has a dirt floor."

Curt just laughed and said, "At this point, I'd believe anything! It figures—you picked it out. You sure got that place cleaned out quick. I'll meet you there tomorrow."

The following day, I met Curt in our potential business establishment. He surveyed the scene, looking at the floor and said, "We have a real problem here. Did you know that the concrete workers' union are on strike? I guess we'll just have to pour the concrete floor ourselves."

This place was turning into a lot of work, but I was up for it. I knew that this was the best option we had, even if it wasn't quite ideal. It seems to be true that you just have to take what you are dealt and make it into what you want. There are a lot of people that never accomplish anything just because they expect everything to be perfect before they get to work. I have found that you have to make your opportunities for success and then it can happen, not the reverse.

THE PRICE OF A CONCRETE FLOOR

After searching for a month, Curt finally found a place that would rent me a dump truck. He gave me directions to the gravel pits where they filled sand, gravel, and portland. I rented the truck, picked it up, and went to the store to meet up with Curt.

Curt was in the passenger seat, giving me directions. We left the service road from the Eden's Expressway after we had passed the concrete pit. We had to take a service road back to the pits. We drove out there and then saw a picket line, blocking the entrance. This was all part of the concrete workers' union's strike and their efforts to halt all construction that used concrete.

Curt gave me some instructions and told me, "Put the pedal to the metal and run those son of a bitches over if they don't get outta the way!"

I downshifted and floored it as I honked the air horn, as a warning, while climbing a steep grade to the gravel pit. The picket line parted, just like the Red Sea.

We made quick time in the pit as we overloaded the truck with gravel, sand, and fifty 100lb. bags of portland. I remember Curt telling me, "Now all we have to do is get outta here." He climbed back into the truck after paying the man. I knew that was easier said than done because the union workers had seen us come in and knew we had to come out. We had been in the pits for a couple hours, and we were sure the union strikers had called for reinforcements.

Curt shared some sage advice with me: "Billy, get it going as fast as you can. We're gonna bust that picket line!"

I began driving the rig much faster than I wanted to with Curt urging me on to get the truck going even faster. We were accelerating downhill now, and, as we were leaving, I saw, off in the distance, the twelve-foot-high chain-linked gates with a union picket line across it. I looked down at the speedometer, and I was doing fifty miles an hour with a dangerously heavy load in the bed of the dump truck. I couldn't have stopped if I'd have wanted to!

Several men on the picket line fired shotguns at the rented truck, hitting the windshield but missing the targeted radiator. Curt stuck his hand out the window with his own pistol, returning fire as we broke through the gates, leaving the pits behind us.

I had to slow down substantially as I exited the gravel pit. We went through a grassy knoll and down over the curb before we ended up on the moderately busy Eden's Expressway. Once we got onto the main road, we headed on to the store. At that point, I started to feel more comfortable with the whole idea Curt had for us.

When we got back to our place, I began backing the truck down the long, seventy-five-foot driveway. There were mere inches of clearance on each side, between the two buildings, as I drove it in reverse. I was relieved when the rig was finally in position to unload. I saw an electric cement mixer in the front of the store, as I came to a stop. Curt commented, "Well at least he came through with the cement mixer."

I dumped the load and returned the truck to the rental place, Pearson's U-Haul, and parked it in the back so that it would be harder to notice the broken windshield. I was lucky they didn't inspect it while I was there. I hurriedly left the lot and drove back to the store.

When I got there, Curt had plugged power into the cement mixer and it was ready to use and rolling. He handed me a garden hose to use to put water in it. That's when he explained to me, "All you have to remember is three, two, one. Three shovels full of sand, two shovels full of gravel, and one shovel full of portland." He showed me how to mix it with the total of six shovels full of materials that he added to the mixer. With that simple instruction, he made a quick departure.

He made a sarcastic remark as he exited saying, "Have fun!" with a smile on his face as he left me to my work.

I filled the mixer with a single load and emptied it into a wheelbarrow and dumped it inside the store, on the floor. I spread it out as far as I could and noticed that I had put a bit too much water in it but figured I had started a good foundation and had done enough for that strenuous, nerve-racking day.

One of the bust-out laborer guys that had helped me clear out the place saw me and asked me if I needed help with the cement. I told him to meet me there early the next day.

The next morning, true to his word, Clayton was there for me. He was a hillbilly kid from Uptown that really worked hard, and I was relieved that he was available to help. As I mixed the cement, he rolled in the wheelbarrow which we loaded to the brim with cement. He dumped it out in evenly spaced drop-off points, covering the building's dirt floor with a rough layer of cement. Every so often, I would stop mixing to smooth out the surface until it had a decent finish.

It took a lot of sweat and effort. I felt like I had a broken back, but we finally finished the job. Every bone in my body ached. We had begun at 6:00 a.m. and didn't get done until the summer sun had set. We parted ways as I gave Clayton $50.00 cash for his time and help.

I crawled into my car, drove home, took a long, hot shower, and stayed in bed for three days straight, only getting up to eat and use the bathroom. I was in some rather severe pain and had worked so hard that it damn near killed me, no thanks to my business partner.

THE STORE TAKES SHAPE

C urt kept on calling me, but I was not answering the phone while I was recovering. On the fourth day, I finally called him at American Bonding, and he said, "I drove by the store and all of the sand, gravel, and portland was gone. Do we need any more?"

I burst out laughing as I said, "No, the last load that I made, I was a little short but I put in two shovels full of dirt to finish it off." He asked me to meet him there so I did.

As I opened the barn doors, he said, "Ya know, you did a nice job here!" as he looked at the floor. "I need a key so I can get in when you're not around."

We walked around on the curing cement floor describing to each other where to build various items we would need for the store. He was also reminding me of an obvious fact, "Red, we still need heat and air conditioning."

By now I knew that Curt's version of the word "we" meant that I would be the one doing all of the work again, but he would be there to provide us with any of the supplies I'd need to finish the job. At least the guy was consistent!

The next week I went to the Montgomery Ward's damaged goods store and bought a five-ton air conditioner that had sealed copper tubing with Freon in it. I, of course, installed all of it by myself, included the forced air ductwork. Curt came by to take a look at it, bringing me a 200 amp Zinsco panel box along with some electrical wire that he procured from Weenie World. Later on that same week, he brought me some unassembled drop-ceiling parts and some stolen light fixtures, which he said fell off a truck. I again enlisted the services of Clayton, the hillbilly kid, to help me wire the lights and various duplex outlets that we needed.

A couple days later I opened the doors to the store and saw a pile of two-by-fours, plywood, and enough Plexiglass to finish the construction of the place. We mapped out the office, a twenty-four inch raised platform counter, a dividing wall that would separate the sales of adult magazines or, as *Chicago Tribune* writer, John Kass, later put it "smut," and a showcase for the 8mm films that I would purchase once things were ready. I replaced the swinging barn doors with a nice, aluminum glass store front, all with the help of Clayton. It was really coming together, and all of the hard work started to show.

Over the next several weeks of construction, a short, thin man in his sixties came by and paid us a visit. He was wearing clean, gray construction-worker pants, and a short-sleeved shirt. He looked around as he surveyed my work simply saying, "Nice." A while later Curt came in to talk to him.

The man said that his name was Marsh, and he would be building the peep shows in the back of the store. The older man brought in a balding forty-eight-year-old, Alva Johnson Rodgers, "Johnny Rodgers," as he called himself.

Rodgers was a real greenhorn when it came to construction but bragged that he could do anything after serving time in Atlanta Federal Prison with Marsh. It was clear to me that he knew nothing about what he was doing. Marsh didn't stick around to see Johnny make a fool out of himself.

Despite Johnny's ignorance and obvious deficiencies, he kept insisting that he knew how to hook up the electricity. Several times throughout our work on the site, I saw him foolishly shock himself, most notable during the assembly of the peep show booths.

In the process of working on the frames for the peep shows, Johnny had somehow managed to get himself caught between two electrical fields! He was receiving 220 volts of current surging through his entire body as he bounced up and down, cracking his chin and then the top of his head on an open hole where the screen for the peep-show would eventually mount. I saw this happening and came to his aid by giving him a solid punch to the head while he was between the frames in order to set him free, for which he genuinely thanked me, as proved by the broad smile on his face.

"Thank God Marsh was not here to see the entertainment," I told him, and he readily agreed with me.

Johnny Rodgers explained that he shared a cell, in prison, with Marsh, AKA Marshall Caifano, the old man that I had seen in the construction outfit a bit earlier. "That's my guy. I got his time cut short from prison, and after he got out, he brought me here to Chicago."

Johnny Rodgers grew up in rural Polk County, Florida, a real hillbilly. Everything he said always came out in a deep southern drawl. He'd been in prison several times for bank robbery and other crimes. He also explained that "his guy" would be splitting the proceeds "menza menza" [the Outfit term for 50/50] from the peep shows with himself, his guy, Curt, and I.

We suddenly had partners again, it was explained to me. When I talked to Curt about it, he told me not to worry because we had the keys to the coin-boxes. "We're going to get our share out of the boxes before he gets to it," Curt assured me. That wasn't exactly what I wanted to hear, but I wasn't surprised to hear it, either. This was Curt's modus operandi, after all, but I wasn't sure it was a good idea to take that kind of an attitude with these new partners of ours—particularly with Caifano.

All this time I made regular reports to John Osborne, my FBI handler by phone, using the code name of my last Company Commander in the Corps, Arthur Zerzow.

WE FINALLY OPEN AND CURT MAKES A MOVE ON ME

We opened the store on Labor Day weekend, and we made a grand total of $13.00. All this despite the fact that "we" were planning on remaining open 24 hours a day, 7 days a week—and had no other employees. It was obvious to me that if we really wanted to make some money, then we were catering to the wrong type of clientele: the heterosexual community. Our store was located between the Bijou Theater, a gay bar, the Glory Hole Tavern, and the Over 21, all of which were gay-themed.

It was very clear to me that we would make a lot more money if we changed things up to cater to the homosexual crowds already frequenting the area. I made some immediate changes in our featured material. After the change-up and refocus, I quickly learned that I had the right business model. Customers and their money immediately poured in, and I salvaged our opening week's bottom line.

Curt told me, "Some of my brother musta rubbed off on you. I'm not gonna run that kinda place!"

We had a real difference of opinions on how things should be run, but I was convinced that we could never turn a profit if we didn't keep with the dramatic changes I was making.

As I explained earlier, Curt had taken a loan out for the materials from his buddy, Francis Carnacle. Unbeknownst to me, Curt had stashed some of the money from the loan away for himself, giving me materials that he procured from Weenie World instead of paying for them. I wondered what he did with the money and later learned that he actually had a noble purpose for the funds, as he desperately tried to cure his ailing sister, Marion.

Curt used the bulk of the money that was supposed to go to business start-up costs to pay for a fruitless trip to the Philippines to procure some VooDoo cancer treatment for Marion. Soon after their return to the states, she passed away. Despite his best efforts, Curt was powerless to do anything to save his sister.

A few days after our fallout in business philosophies, Curt told me I was out of the business and to stay away from the store. I had the only combination to the safe and all of the keys to the coin-boxes. When I left, he had no way of taking any money from the store, and he hadn't realized that fact until it was too late.

Over the course of the following weeks, Curt threatened to kill me several times. We had constant arguments about how to manage and run the store. He even fired several shots at me under the L-tracks right next to police headquarters. None of the police paid any attention, and given our ties to organized crime, I knew I was on my own to deal with this situation.

Curt wanted those keys and the combination to the safe, and he was very willing to kill me to get them. Another associate of mine named Lenny was behind the counter when Curt came in with "Big Bob" Davids, a mountain of a man that stood 6' 8" and weighed well over 300 lbs. He picked Lenny up by his throat, lifting him over the counter, and said, "This ain't no leg-breakin' situation, I just wanna get ahold of Red." Curt approvingly watched the exchange from a couple of feet away.

Lenny called me on the phone, telling me that they were holding a gun to his head, and that if I didn't come down there right then, they were going to kill him. I told Lenny, "Don't worry, they're not gonna kill ya, you're the only one that knows how to reach me." Lenny was scared, so he said to them, "Look, I just work here. Can you pay me, and I will leave?"

I knew better than to give in, and Curt finally left the store, disappointed. Lenny was more than a bit shaken, but he was otherwise no worse for wear.

I moved from motel to motel for a time, checking in with Lenny through my pager as I stayed on the move in order to keep everyone safe. Sometime later I called Lenny from Marina City, from a restaurant payphone. He told me that Curt just wanted to talk to me and that he was at American Bonding and I should call him there.

THE DRIVE

I called American Bonding and talked to Curt. He told me that he didn't want any more trouble and we could straighten everything out.

I told him, "No way, I'm tired of you shooting at me!"

He chuckled and said, "That's over. We have to put the business back together. Business comes first."

I didn't trust a word he said. He told me, "Look, meet me across the street from American Bonding. I'll be alone. We can go for a drive in your car and talk it out." I told him I'd be there in about half an hour.

When I showed up to pick up Curt for our ride and negotiations, there were hundreds of people around us, and I asked him to get into the car. Curt got in and should have known he was in for it when he saw that I had on a motorcycle helmet and my driving gloves! Squealing my tires in my '73 Oldsmobile down State Street, we were drifting sideways as I made a left-hand turn onto Balboa Drive.

Curt kept telling me to slow down. I headed for Lakeshore Drive at approximately sixty miles an hour. We were running through red lights, turning on s-curves where the speed limit was twenty miles an hour. Curt was doing all he could to hold onto the car for dear life! I turned off an exit on Addison Avenue into a parking lot and slammed on the brakes, turning the car sideways as we skidded to a halt.

"All those times you threatened to kill me, I'm only gonna tell ya one time: keep it up and I'm the one that's gonna kill you," I told Curt. He was breathing heavily and got out of the car. I left him there in the parking lot and drove off, with the keys and combination still safely in my possession and in my mind.

PARTNER SWAP

After dropping off Curt, I went straight to The Red Fox Inn, where Marshall Caifano frequented. I parked in the lot and went in to see him. He was sitting at the bar as I approached him, in genuine anger. I walked up to him and threw all sets of the store keys onto the bar, saying, "You call yourself a man of honor? I'm through with you people!"

Marshall didn't react to my accusations at all, and he tried to calm me down and asked me to take a seat to have a drink with him. He obviously knew nothing about the way Curt had been trying to kill me and take over the store.

"No thanks." And I headed towards the door.

On my way to the exit, two large men picked me up off of my feet and carried me back to a smiling Johnny Marshall [AKA Marshall Caifano]. They let go of me as he said with a grin, "Come on, sit down and have a drink with me. Calm down."

I again headed towards the exit and the same two guys brought me back with my feet off of the ground. He said, a bit exasperatedly, "Are you going to sit down or not?"

So I sat down on the barstool next to him.

The bartender came over and Marshall said, "What are ya drinkin'?"

"Gimme a shot of Scotch with a water back." The bartender poured it for me, and I quickly drank the shot and got up to leave.

The same two bruisers brought me back to sit down on the barstool where I saw Marshal with an even bigger smile, laughing. He said, "Do you want another drink?"

"Ya."

The barkeep poured me another. It was now crystal clear to me that Marsh wasn't going to let me leave without his permission.

I sat down next to him, and he asked me why I was so upset. I told him Curt had taken over the store and was trying to kill me. The grin left his face as I swallowed my Scotch, followed by the water back.

He then asked me what had happened. I told him that Curt had taken over the store and told me to stay out of it. I also told him that Curt intended to steal a little money off of the top of the coin-boxes, but he couldn't do that now because I had just given him the ring of keys.

Marshall and I sat and talked for a few hours. He calmed me down as he bought me several drinks. He stood up and said, "Follow me."

We made our way to a pay phone in the lounge's foyer. When we got to the phone, he put in a dime and told me to dial Curt's number for him. I told him that Curt went to sleep early, and if I awoke him, he'd be very angry.

"Just do as you're told."

I dialed Curt's phone number, at his home, and Marshall snatched the phone receiver out of my hand before I had finished dialing.

I heard Marshall say, "Yeah, it's me. Meet me on the corner of..." as he put his hand over the receiver, he asked me where the nearest restaurant to the store was. I told him it was the Stagecoach. Marshall continued his talk with Curt, "...at the corner, the Stagecoach, you know the place?"

He then hung up the phone without waiting for Curt's response. He told me, "We'll go in your car. Come on." We left to see how things were going at the store. We were followed by the two large men, in another car.

When we got to my store, with snowflakes falling, we all got out, and Marshall started for the corner of the Stagecoach restaurant, down the street. I remember looking at the short, thin, old man walking alone down the street. He was certainly not what he appeared!

The other two men told me, "Come on, Red, we're going in there." gesturing at my business.

I said, "No way, he's got a double-barreled sawed off shotgun!"

One of the bruisers chuckled at me and said, "You've got nothing to be afraid of: you're with us!" I told them I didn't want to go in anyway, so they went into the store without me.

A few moments later a pickup truck came out of the driveway with a man and a girl in it, leaving in a fury. After that exit, one of Marshall's big guys named "Dick" told me to come on in. It appeared they had successfully cleared the place, and there was no one else in the store.

I cautiously entered, and we went into the office. I opened up the safe and all the money was there, just like I had left it. We started to empty the coin boxes and count the money on the plush carpet floor of the office, placing the quarters in $10.00 stacks.

There was a knock on the door, and Dick went to answer it. He came back with Marshall, and they both came into the office. Marshall saw us counting the coins as I asked what happened with Curt. He told me never to ask him again.

As the night went on, we had around $1,000.00 in quarters. Marshall told me, "$500 for you and $500 for me, that's the way it always will be. I don't care how much money you take in, you owe me $500 every week, whether you make $100 a week or $10,000."

He then took me aside and said, "But you have to promise me something: If that guy calls you or bothers you, you have to get ahold of me right away." Just as he was talking to me, the phone rang.

It was Curt, he was breathing heavy, saying, "Billy, what are you doing? You almost got me killed right here in the restaurant!"

As he finished his sentence, I told him, "Curt, someone is here with me, and I promised that if you ever called me or contacted me, I would tell him." I heard the click of the receiver as Curt hurriedly hung up.

Marshall told me, "Remember that promise. It was him, wasn't it?" I told him it was, but when he heard what I said, he'd hung up as quickly as he could.

Marshall told me it was my store now: mine and mine alone. I cashed in his quarters for $20 bills and gave them to him. He told me that Rodgers would be handling the money pick-ups for us and that he trusted me to get his share right each time so Roger wouldn't be coming in to count it.

"Just make sure you have an envelope of $500 for him each week." I told him I understood. Marsh and his bodyguards got in their car and drove off while I finished things at the store before going home for the night.

The next day I called and briefed my FBI handler, John Osborne, on the events that had taken place. He was impressed and encouraged me to keep up the great work. He also said he was going to be transferring to Philadelphia. He said that someone he trusted from his unit, "The Mob Squad," would handle me from now on. I met with both of them, and my new handler was S/A Hank Schmidt. Hank was a transplant from Oklahoma and much younger than John.

Mañana Never Comes

Kenny called me while all of these things were taking place and asked me to meet him, Curt, and Francis Carnacle for dinner. Kenny became involved because Curt couldn't call me himself. I sent my employee, Lenny, as my representative. They ate at a really posh restaurant, and Francis picked up the bill. They had discussed how he was going to collect on his loan.

Curt had told him that he was out of everything, and he'd have to take up the matter with me. Lenny suggested that he talk to Marshall, but Carnacle insisted that he needed to talk to me about it. A few threats were exchanged, and they finished their meal and left. Lenny told me about it after he got home, and we both laughed about the situation.

A couple of days later, I was contacted by phone. It was Francis Carnacle, the guy who had loaned Curt the money for the supplies and construction of the store, and I knew that he wanted his money. My point to him was the fact that I had never borrowed it from him, as my part of the deal was the work and Curt was the one that procured the loan so he would have to take up the matter directly with Curt. He told me that he simply followed the money and that led him to the store.

When he asked me to meet him at the Paul Bunyan restaurant, several doors down from my shop, I didn't have much of a chance to answer because he hung up on me. My father arrived there on my behalf and saw him up against the interior walls of the restaurant, just outside of the washrooms. A Chicago Police Sergeant was also there with two of his officers. They were just finishing up a thorough search of Francis and his two sons, and even though they were searched for weapons and IDs, they couldn't find either. It was clear that they were up to no good, but there was no solid evidence for the officers to use as proof.

My father jammed a .38 caliber revolver into Francis' ribs saying, "Don't you ever try to harm my son!" The police officers overlooked the entire exchange and never mentioned the fact that they saw my father's pistol as they released the men. My dad returned. Francis and his crew also left the scene.

Shortly after the incident, Francis left me a message on my Phone Mate answering machine saying, "Flowers baby, flowers mañana." He never said his name, but I could tell it was him. Needless to say, mañana never came, and he never got his money back nor did I ever hear from him again. Rest assured that every one of these not so friendly exchanges and events that I was involved with were reported in full detail to the FBI.

ON MY OWN—WITH MARSHALL

I now knew I was completely free to run the store exactly as I wanted to so I made a few significant changes. The next day I started hiring gay people to work the counter and their loyal patrons followed.

Naturally, as was later quoted by several judges and newspapers, I couldn't hire people that were bankers or other legitimate businessmen, so I wound up hiring what I called "the dregs of society." They were genuine freaks and all of them had criminal backgrounds. I paid them $2.50 an hour. They were cheap help in every sense of the word. Most of them stole from me, even under the threat that they knew it was a "connected joint." I also expanded store operations as I installed my own cigarette vending machine, a Pepsi can machine, and a few pinball machines. I retained all of the profits I made from them—unlike other "connected" businesses where the Outfit owned and operated the vending machines and only returned a token margin to the business owners.

One time a police officer came to my home and told me that one of my employees on the afternoon shift, Dan Peak, was selling cocaine over the counter in the store. The DEA eventually arrested him at his home after I dropped a dime on him. Despite some drawbacks like those, business was good, and I obtained an Adult P.P.A. [Public Place of Amusement] license and changed the business name from "The Peeping Tom" to "Chicago's Old Town Video."

Between my own aforementioned Pepsi machine, cigarette machine, and a few pinball machines in the store, I'd pocket fifty grand every two weeks, not including what the store itself made. One of my other business ventures came from California. We called it "RUSH." It was a product that was a vascular dilator, the twist was that instead of using amyl alcohol

I manufactured it using n-butyl alcohol that was classified as a chemical, unlike amyl alcohol which was classified as a drug. That was how I avoided manufacturing scrutiny by federal authorities and kept it cheap and profitable.

People used to inhale it from a one-dram bottle instead of using a prescription package of poppers—like what is used to awaken someone who has lost consciousness. These were very popular with the crowd I serviced as they would use them in an effort to enhance and gratify their sexual experiences. I also manufactured a generic version I labeled "Dr. Popper" which was the same stuff just under a different label.

After a while, that one business alone was so good that I manufactured seven or eight bottles of the same product under different names and distributed them nationwide. This continued up until Johnny Rodgers wanted me to buy him out of his half of the peep shows for a meager $1,500.00. I readily complied and got him his money.

Rodgers was taking $250.00 of the $500.00 I was providing to Marshall from the weekly envelopes. All I had to do now was come up with $250.00 a week for Caifano and half of the net proceeds from RUSH. This was very profitable for me.

I went to my factory one day, and Johnny Rodgers said, "My guy told me this business is mine now. Don't come around here anymore."

With that, I lost my 150-gallon Pfaudler reactor and my bottling filler that kicked out a gross of bottles every six minutes. I wasn't happy with the new arrangement, but when he told me "his guy" was involved, I knew he meant Marshall Caifano so I didn't complain. I stayed away from the factory and never asked what their plans were for the place.

I later learned that Johnny Rodgers was making bootleg Quaaludes from my equipment. His operation was forbiddingly illegal, as it constituted the manufacture and distribution of prescription strength drugs without a license, oversight, or approval from the government. That activity alone would have gotten him killed if Joey would have known about it!

After it was all said and done, I had made my money back, and then some, from the equipment. I focused on that fact as I left him to his own devices, sure to keep myself clear of his new, illicit activities.

MY AGORAPHOBIA

In 1973, I was eating breakfast in a restaurant and began to feel uncontrollably dizzy. The waitress came over to me and told me to put my head between my knees and that it might help. It didn't, it only made things worse. My heart was pounding. I was so dizzy that I could barely make it to the washroom, where I cupped my hands and flushed my face with cold water.

A few minutes later, I returned to my seat. Things seemed to be okay as the waitress brought me my breakfast. As I started to eat, I became disoriented with the very same symptoms. I left the restaurant, leaving most of my food behind, and asked Lenny to take me to the nearest hospital. Instead, he drove me home.

I slept until the following day, and I seemed to feel better, as though nothing had ever happened. About a month later, I had the same kind of attack. They kept getting increasingly frequent until 1975. This time, I was not far from Northwestern Memorial Hospital, and they rushed me there in an ambulance after I called for it.

I thought that I was having a heart attack as I complained to the EMT about chest pains, dizziness, and shortness of breath. They attached all kinds of monitoring wires to my chest on the way to the hospital, and by the time we arrived, they had five or six staff members waiting there that rolled me into the emergency room.

Several doctors examined me. They were looking at the monitoring machines and the data they recorded. I was scared. About an hour later, they rolled me into a private room, just off from the others. A young doctor came into the room, and after a few moments of questions, he gave me an injection and left. All kinds of crazy thoughts were racing through my mind, and I was absolutely sure that I was going to die!

About fifteen minutes later, the same young doctor returned to my room, asking me how I felt. I suddenly determined that things weren't as bad as I thought as I asked him if it was okay for me to sit up.

"Sure, if you feel like it," he said, with a smile on his face.

I sat up and felt very relaxed and reflective as I inventoried my thoughts and feelings.

Seconds later, I asked him if it would be okay to walk, and he replied, again, "If you feel like it."

As I walked across the room in a euphoric condition, he asked me if I had been under a lot of stress lately. I replied, "You might say that!" as I reflected on my many frustrations associated with Curt Hansen, the building of the bookstore, and my double life as an FBI informant with the Outfit.

"By the way, what was in that shot that you gave me?" I asked, hoping it had just cured me. He told me that it was Valium, and I was never so embarrassed in all of my life. Here I had thought that I was dying from something serious and all I needed was a shot of tranquilizer.

I immediately walked over, as quickly as I could, to pay my bill for the hospital visit and got out of there. As I was leaving, the young doctor suggested that I see a psychiatrist. For some reason I implicitly trusted his judgment.

These panic attacks continued and got more and more frequent and increasingly severe. I began to notice that they were occurring every day. It got to the point where I never left my home. I had them anytime, anywhere, and I was just better equipped to deal with them in the privacy of my own residence, so I stayed home.

When I checked in with the FBI, by phone, Hank Schmidt wanted to meet me at a restaurant. I told him that I simply couldn't and he asked me why. He said, "We need to get you some help, Red." I told him that I had already called a number of psychiatrists, but all of them wanted me to go to their offices—and that was something that I just couldn't do. I was frustrated beyond belief.

John Osborne called me and asked me if I knew of any psychiatrist that I trusted. I told him about this young doctor that had treated me in the Emergency Room at Northwestern Memorial Hospital. Several days later, I received a call from that very doctor who asked me if I had sought treatment since my visit to the ER.

I said, "No, I haven't left the house in over a year."

He told me, "Well, we'll have to do something about that. When do you want me to come over and see you?"

I laughingly told him to pick a day because I would always be there.

He chuckled and said, "How about Tuesday evening at about 7 o'clock?"

"Fine. By the way, why did you call *me*?"

He told me that he had been contacted by an FBI agent by the name of John Osborne who had told him to reach out to me. John had told me that everything we discussed was secure and confidential because of our doctor/patient relationship. That made me feel very comfortable.

I continued to see him for several years, speaking to him of my most intimate thoughts and secrets, all in an attempt to get well. He even tried several medications that had horrific side effects on me. Several times he came over on the weekends, and he would attempt to take me out on somewhat of a field trip, where he could observe my panic attacks as they happened.

He saw me twice a week in the evenings. We drank Scotch together and talked about the problems of each other's day. Eventually, he gave me a book to read called *The Anxiety Disease*. After reading it, I believed that there was hope of recovering.

He prescribed another medication for me, although I refused to take it. I had become phobic of medicine because of the many side effects that I had previously endured.

One evening, he came over to my house and stayed there with a pill and glass of water in his hand until I took it. I paced the floor thinking terrible thoughts like, what if this is cyanide?

He was amused as he watched me with a smile on his face, until I finally told him that it was okay to leave. He increased the dosage of my medication over a period of time until I reached what he referred to as "a blocking dosage."

We had found the right medication for me, and I was now able to leave my house and function normally in my day to day activities. I was finally feeling more mobile, owing to the effects of my medication, and I had a new lease on life. This took place somewhere around 1986.

* * *

I have often thought, "What a great doctor and friend. He really cared." Looking back, I see a great man who I will never forget until I draw my last breath. I could have never lived the life I led without his help. Now how do you put a price on that? I owe him my life.

THE SAD TALE OF
DANIEL SEIFERT

There were a lot of business dealings that the Outfit had their hands in and the fiberglass shop, Plastic-Matic Products, that Danny Seifert had been running was no exception. Money laundering enterprises were a real necessity for the Mob, and they took advantage of their connections to legitimate businesses for illegitimate scheming.

Things were going well for Danny, but they came to a grinding halt once he was indicted for income tax evasion and racketeering. Danny didn't want to go to prison so he became a cooperating government witness, willing to testify against all Outfit members involved in the kickback scheme from the Teamster's Pension Fund Loan, which had funded Circus Circus Casino in Las Vegas. His willingness to work with federal authorities put his life and family in real danger. He made no bones about it: he was going to testify, and he told his connected benefactors of his intentions to become a cooperative witness for the feds. His brother, a mob-bookie, tried to talk him out of it, and even Joey Lombardo himself had tried to talk him out of it on numerous occasions—but Danny had made up his mind and that was that.

Early one morning when Danny was opening up the factory with his wife and youngest son, Joe (named after Lombardo, I should mention), a terribly predictable murder occurred. Joey Lombardo, wearing a ski mask, forced Danny's wife and six-year old son into a bathroom as Frankie took care of Danny, firing several shots at him.

Danny fled through the parking lot, wounded, and Frankie followed him until he fell. Frank finished the job as he shot him in the head with a double-barreled shotgun, at point blank range, killing him on the spot.

The set-up for Daniel Seifert's murder was all part of an elaborate plan. As local police officers received word of shots being fired at the factory, they proceeded to the scene without delay. The Outfit used several "block cars" that were crashed into any Bensenville police cruisers that were called to the sight and thus allowed plenty of time for the deed to be done and a clean escape for the perpetrators.

Later that night, coverage of the crime was on every news channel, showing a police composite-image that looked like the artist had invited Joey Lombardo to the session to pose as his model while he made a charcoal sketch. A lot of people knew what had happened, but it takes a lot more than knowledge to make a case end up in court. Joey remained a free man, along with Frankie, and the other guys involved in the hit.

Danny's family suffered dearly as the government confiscated everything that his immediate family owned, causing a great hardship on his wife and children. His sons, Nick and Joey, had it particularly hard in that they couldn't make many friends after that incident.

Since there isn't a collateral victim's fund to help families affected by court case fallout, the Seiferts were victimized once by the Mob and then again by the government. Unfortunately, their story was pretty typical for the time and contributed to the prevailing notion that coming forth to the feds, when the Outfit was involved, was a very bad idea. There is nothing more effective in teaching a lesson than providing an example, and the Seifert family's situation was pitiable in every way.

Danny's murder ended the government's case against the Outfit members because there was no one left to testify against them—and thus the Mob's reputation for intimidation and being able to get away with anything they pleased was openly enhanced. Once by not having to go to a court proceeding and again by virtue of the fact that everyone knew the reason why: they had disposed of yet another witness prior to the trial. A win-win opportunity had presented itself to them, and the Outfit had cashed in a former member's chips.

I never would have guessed, at the time of these events, that Nick Seifert, Danny's oldest boy, and I would become good friends. We came into contact with each other after I had testified in the Family Secrets Trial in 2007. We spoke many times as I explained to him how JL had actually saved his mother and younger brother's lives during the contract murder. I told him, "If Joey would have wanted your mother dead, it would have made things a lot easier for him; however, I think he spared her life because he did, indeed, try and talk your father out of testifying—on numerous occasions." Nick confirmed that with me, telling me that his uncle, the Mob bookmaker, also had tried to dissuade his father from testifying. I told Nick a lot of things. We had some very interesting conversations. I still consider him a close friend, certainly someone I would trust. Incidentally, John J. Flood, a former Cook County police officer who I came into contact with in 1989, is the man who put us in touch with one another.

THE BOYS MOVE IN

A couple of thugs, Pete "The Greek" Dounis, Babe DeMonte, Joseph "Little Caesar" Devarco, and Johnny Matasa, AKA "Pudgy," put the muscle on the gay bar next to my store to pay street tax. The owner of the tavern was named Bob Hugel, and he had done me a favor back when he had given me the name of my landlord, Sam Napaderno, when I was trying to set up the porn shop. When I heard about his problems, I called him to help him negotiate with the Outfit. He told me, "I already have it handled, don't get involved. You're just gonna get into trouble."

I got off of the phone with Bob and seconds later my phone rang. It was Hank Schmidt from the FBI, my current handler. He and John Osborne had been termed my "handlers" as I would only talk to them. If anyone wanted me to talk to another agent from the FBI or another federal agency, my handler would call me and then conference the call, never giving up my name or contact information to *anyone*. They later referred other federal agencies to me, as in the case of a U.S. Postal Inspection Service investigation with Steve Toushin.

Hank was angry with me for calling Bob. He then told me that Bob had contacted the FBI Organized Crime Unit, telling them that he would testify to what had happened. The FBI told him he needed to liquidate his assets in order for them to help protect him. He would sell his tavern to a gay couple named Bill Blair and Berry McDermitt.

Bob Hugel went into the witness protection program prior to the trial. The thugs were out on bond until the trial, nearly two years later. They were charged with violation of "The Hobbs Act" [extortion]. After their trial, Pete went to prison. Matasa and Caesar Devarco beat the rap.

Bob Hugel had done his duty and was now out of the picture and living in Denver, where the Federal Marshals had relocated him. Assistant U.S. Attorney John Scully had successfully prosecuted the case.

* * *

Berry and Bill, the new owners of the bar next door to me, were gay lovers. Berry's mother, Zoe Black, who lived in Brooklyn, New York, loaned them the money for the bar, and they agreed to pay her back the $50,000 it took to take over operations. I got along with them just fine, and business was good for all of us.

One of the new owners of the bar, Bill Blair, contacted me by phone and wanted to know if I could procure a 4:00 a.m. liquor license for him, as Bob Hugel had when he owned the place. Those were really hard to get unless you had connections downtown—like me or my associates. When Bob sold the bar, he sold it to a legally recognized corporation with Bill and Berry as fifty percent stockholders. Despite their repeated efforts, they could only get a 2:00 a.m. license. Having that extra two hours could increase your profits by double.

I contacted Lt. Green, head of the liquor license unit of the Chicago Police. He told me they could have the license for $1,500 but to make sure I tacked on at least the same amount for my own pocket. They got their late license, and Bill drove out to my home and paid me $1,500 in hundred dollar bills. I never tacked on a fee for myself.

Three weeks after procuring the license, Berry came to my house all beaten up and said Bill had kicked him out of the apartment above the bar, where they both lived. Bill told him he would have to leave and find his own place to live, as he had found himself a younger man to replace him—but he promised he would pay Berry for it.

Bill never came up with any money for Berry, and Berry still owed his mother the $50 Grand that they borrowed to buy the bar and lease for the apartment that the deal had included. Both of these guys knew, by now, that I had strong ties with both the Outfit and the Chicago Police.

All that Berry wanted to do now was destroy Bill Blair, as he didn't see his mother or him ever getting back any money from his former lover. Berry told me, "I want to sell you my 50% of the stock for $10.00 and bust Bill Blair out." I told him I wouldn't do that, but what I would do was buy the stock for $10.00 and become Blair's partner, giving him half of everything I collected from Bill.

Berry signed over his 50% of the stock in my office seconds later, with a Bill of Sale that we had notarized. Then I called Bill Blair, on a speakerphone, so Berry could hear what was said. I asked him how business was doing and he told me, "Very well now that we have the 4:00 a.m. license."

I told him I wanted to know because I wanted to see how my partner was doing. Bill was confused by my statement and asked me, "What do you mean?" I told him that Berry had sold me his half of the bar.

Bill started screaming at me saying, "He can't do that, I have first right of refusal!"

I told him, "I don't see that written here. Now do you want to come to see me tomorrow, or do you want me to come to see you?"

The next day, Bill came to see me and brought the books from the business and some money for me. He came every Monday to see me for several weeks and would bring me my half of the money that the bar took in, showing me his expenses. I agreed to stay out of the bar as long as he kept his word. That was the terms of our partnership—and Bill readily agreed to it.

Over the course of the next months, Berry and his mother got their money back, and more, and everything had worked out between us. I also secured a new liquor license with both our names on it, as I was now a full partner with Bill Blair. Berry then faded out of the picture and left everyone alone after he moved back to New York.

Several months later, I came upon some unfortunate news one day when one of our bartenders called me. He informed me that Bill was making false receipts to show me so that he could pocket the difference. The City of Chicago Liquor License was due to be renewed on November 1st of that year. On October 31st, late that night after a big Halloween bash, the bar was closed. I went down to the bar and saw Bill making up false receipts as he sat by the cash register, drunk.

He laughed and told me, "So you caught me. What are you going to do, kill me?!" I just walked over to the framed liquor license and took it off the wall and smashed it on the bar, telling him, "Have fun getting it renewed without me."

A few days later I filed a civil lawsuit against him for dissolution of business. He hired an attorney after he was served with the papers. His attorney told my attorney that I could buy him out for $50,000 or his half of the business. I just laughed at the offer and called Bill's attorney to discuss the arrangements.

He told me that he couldn't talk to me, he could only talk to my attorney that represented me. That's when I conferenced a call to Howie Gilman, my attorney, telling him that Bill's attorney was on the line with us and I wanted to waive the client privilege.

Howie chuckled and said, "Yea, you guys can talk any time you want!" and then hung up.

I told Bill's lawyer, "I'll tell you what: your client can buy me out for the $50,000." I'm sure he knew that I certainly wasn't going to buy him out at that price.

He then told me that his client wasn't interested in buying me out because he wanted me to buy him out so he wouldn't go for that. As he started to say his goodbye, I told him, "Now don't hang up, because if you do, after you hang up, the price for his half drops to $25,000."

He laughed at my comments and said, "Okay, I'll talk to Bill." and hung up, not taking me seriously.

Several weeks later he called me back and said, "I talked to Bill, and he wants you to buy him out."

I told him, "I have no interest in that deal, but right now the price is $25,000. Don't hang up because if you do, the next time we speak the price is $12,500."

He thought I was joking as I refreshed his memory about the last call we had.

When he hung up the phone, I called Howie and told him to call the Cook County State's Attorney's Office and file a criminal complaint for embezzlement. He did just that and served Bill's attorney. After cutting the price down in half every time I talked to Bill's lawyer, I went to $6,250 and stopped there once he told me that I was being ridiculous. Bill's lawyer then told me his client would consider selling me his half for $25,000.

I told him, "Now my offer is nothin'. Your client never paid the rent and was evicted from the apartment above the bar...and the landlord wanted me to pay the rent. I told him I wouldn't pay as long as Bill didn't pay his half."

His lawyer didn't have much to say at that point, so I hung up.

I had told the landlord, "If you have any ideas of renting it, I will see you in court and serve you with a restraining order until my matter is settled with the state's attorney's office." He must have known I was serious so he didn't do anything to contest me.

I spoke again with Bill's lawyer. He told me his client was broke and didn't know how he was going to pay his fee. I told him, "That's a Y.P. not a M.P.: your problem, not my problem. Bill's going to jail, and I'm just the guy that's goin' to put him there."

His attorney didn't have much to say after that, but I was sure that he knew me well enough by now to know that I was not one to bluff.

Not long after that conversation, Bill's attorney and I settled things out of court. I would assume the bills owed on the hard booze and beer. I would just take possession of the place, dropping the criminal charges against his client. This dissolved our partnership, without my having to go after either Bill or his lawyer, and I became the sole owner.

* * *

I put my father on the liquor license, just as I did at the bookstore, P.P.A. ([Adult]Public Place of Amusement) and opened the bar up again with a late night license, owing to the further help from my political connections. I hired a gay manager and a few gay bartenders who had a local following. We reopened and the place was an immediate success as business was booming.

Sometime later the owner of the building itself, James Corbett, called me. He slurred his words, as he was drunk, and asked me, "Do you wanna buy the building? I want outta this."

I told him, "Jay, you got nothing to worry about. Nobody is gonna hurt ya. I'll be the best tenant you ever had."

I really didn't want to buy the building at that time, but he made me an offer I couldn't refuse: I bought the building, with him financing it, and the mortgage payment was less than the payment on the lease. I ended up giving him more than it was worth, at the time of the sale, and we were both happy with the terms.

With the proceeds from the bar, I paid off the building in two years, while I lived in the second story apartment, free and clear of rent. Not long after my purchase of that building, I made another real estate deal and lived above the bar while I made my other holding into what I really wanted.

Less than a year after I began my original bookstore lease with Sam Napaderno, he passed away, leaving the property to his adopted daughter, Mary O'Keefe. She lived in River Forest, Illinois, an affluent western suburb which was just over the Chicago city limit's dividing line. She worked for Cook County, until she retired. She told me she would sell me the bookstore building once the lease was up for $75,000.00.

After procuring a construction loan for the place, I paid Mary off and remodeled the top half of the building, adding a third floor, giving me two full floors of residence.

Above the bookstore was my living room, dining room, kitchen, laundry room, a large fireplace, bathroom with an enormous shower, and a three sink vanity with a mirror that ran its length. A full service wet bar was built into the wall. At the push of a button, the doors to it slid open, and a soda machine was also on tap so that any of my guests could drink whatever they wanted. I also had two oversized living room sets with couches, loveseats, chairs and ottomans along with a concert grand piano, all in an effort to occupy the immense area. There was a full service dining room that could sit and serve ten people, next to the kitchen. I had the largest refrigerator that could be bought at that time, and I employed a full-time maid. The laundry room was accessed through the kitchen and ran parallel to the bathroom and had a large sized washer and dryer set.

The pitched roof was taken out to make way for the four top floor bedrooms, and a flat tar and felt roof was added in its place. My master bedroom had two king-sized beds and was at the front of the building so I had three windows that let in plenty of natural light. The master bedroom faced the street and had its own bathroom. The three remaining bedrooms shared the other bathroom, and I made one of them into a full service office with all the copy machines, printers, computers, and other high end technology devices available at the time.

I have always liked quality art work. I filled the place with paintings, lithographs and other fine art pieces that adorned my walls and tables.

I had five separate phone lines on a Merlin system, giving me access to four lines and an intercom. One of the lines, my private, secure line, actually went to another address down the alley and was exclusively used for my calls with the FBI or other private matters.

The place was built like Fort Knox and was very secure, with walls that were a foot and a half thick at the top with bases that were more than three feet wide.

Less than five years later, I sold the same building for $500,000.00. Needless to say, Mary wasn't happy about it and the fact that she could've asked for more when she sold it to me. The businesses paid both of the properties off, leaving me with a large income and a few million in real estate equity. Business was good, and my bottom line certainly proved it.

Marshall Caifano and Ray Ryan

Raymond J. Ryan was a prominent Palm Springs real estate developer and businessman who had a partnership with William Holden and several other movie stars, establishing the Mount Kenya Safari Club in Kenya, Africa. He had also made millions upon millions of dollars from mineral rights' leases on farms in the Midwest.

He purchased mineral rights on farmlands in Indiana, Illinois, Iowa, and surrounding states. The farmers were thinking that he was looking for oil. He did find some oil, but he hit the real pay dirt there in the form of natural gas. This exceeded his wealth earned from all of the oil wells that he had drilled in Texas and Oklahoma. Between his real estate and all of his energy producing activities, he had made more than enough money to live very comfortably for the rest of his life.

I learned about Ray Ryan's dealings with the Outfit from the mouth of Marshall Caifano himself. Marshall told me that Ray Ryan had sent him to prison because he and Johnny Del Monaco sat in the back of his limo with him. Ray had been a frequent and very degenerate gambler in Las Vegas and had some very heavy gambling debts.

He had taken juice loans to pay them off, and Marsh had been sent to collect on them and set the terms of his payout. He had owed about $850,000.00, but that was enough money to warrant a hit on him. They had promised Ray Ryan that if he would give them a million dollars every year, then they would let him live.

When the car slowed to a stop, Ray jumped out of his limo, right in the middle of Palm Springs, California, and ran to the nearest payphone. He called the FBI to volunteer some very helpful information to them if they would prosecute the men who were threatening his life. The Feds took him up on the offer.

A while later Marshall was indicted and convicted along with Johnny Del Monaco, for the extortion of Ray Ryan. He was then sentenced to serve time in Atlanta Federal Penitentiary where he celled with Johnny Rodgers, whom several FBI agents referred to as Marshall's "prison wife." Rodgers helped him procure an early release. Marshall went after Ryan, with Joey Lombardo's permission. He was out for revenge as Ray Ryan, in his estimate, had taken several years of his life from him.

In 1977, Ray had just finished one of his workouts at an Evansville, Indiana, health club he frequented and got into his Lincoln Mark V to leave. As he started the car, it violently exploded, sending pieces of the vehicle hundreds of feet in every direction and killing the man almost instantly. At least that's what the police report read. Although a suspect, Marshall was never arrested for the bombing.

I was somewhat shocked at the news of Ryan's death because Johnny Rodgers had been playing with my remote control device when I was installing it on my garage door opener. He was trying to see if an 18-volt garage door opener could be powered by a 12-volt auto battery and detonate a blasting cap. This gave me somewhat of an insight and suspicion as to how the murder occurred—by use of a garage door opener, detonated remotely—despite the news reports that a bomb was connected directly to the ignition. The murder remains an open case to this day, but I think it is clear who did it. Johnny Rodgers' debriefing with Hank Schmidt of the FBI confirmed those facts.

Johnny Rodgers Story

Johnny Rodgers' real name was Alva Johnson Rodgers. He told me that his mother named him that after his biological father, a Pentecostal preacher named, Alva Johnson, with whom she'd had an affair. He was born and raised in Kissimmee, Florida, in Polk County.

He claimed to be a natural-born pyromaniac, telling me that at eight years old, his parents bought him a chemistry set, and he blew up their barn and burned it to the ground with a chemical concoction he devised. That was his first run in with the law.

He was in and out of juvenile detention throughout his youth owing to the many fires he'd start and that was what he had instead of a formal education. Later on in his life, amongst other criminal ventures, he graduated to grand theft auto and bank robbery.

The guys in the Grand Avenue Crew always referred to him as "The Hillbilly" because of his deep southern drawl, rural upbringing, low moral values, and obvious lack of education. He was never really accepted by the crew but everyone tolerated him because Marshall brought him.

When I first met Rodgers, while building my store, I noticed that he was driving a brand new Cadillac Eldorado with Florida license plates on it. Marshall Caifano had given him the money to lease it upon his release, on parole, from the Atlanta Federal Penitentiary.

As formally uneducated as he was, he would spend all his free time in prison reading law books which made him into what we referred to as a "jailhouse lawyer." As a result of his learnings, he was able to appeal Marshall's prison time by several years and helped to get him out early.

He would refer to himself as being "his boy," and that Marshall was "his guy." They were cellmates and documented as prison lovers. He even openly confirmed this fact to me and others around me.

The guy had no shame whatsoever and was involved in several bisexual relationships over the years—sometimes just to avoid doing jail time. He was genuinely proud of the crimes he had committed throughout his lengthy career and even testified of that fact under oath in Federal Court in the Family Secrets trial.

Attorney Rick Halprin, Family Secrets Trial

Under cross examination, Rick Halprin, Joey Lombardo's lawyer, had labeled him a "bust out loser" to which Rodgers responded, "I did eleven years for bank robbery, is that heavy enough?" as he grinned and chuckled.

Rick replied with a follow up comment, "I'm glad you're not modest. The bank robbery is probably the highlight of your career?" which Rodgers confirmed by saying, "Well, sort of." The guy was one strange nut to crack, but at least he was forthright!

In reality, Rodgers got away with very few crimes. It seemed that he was nearly always caught.

For example, he robbed a bank in New Jersey and broke into a house that was vacant in order to hide. It all happened on a snowy winter's night. The flakes were falling so fast, he thought his footprints would be covered by the fresh storm.

He was right about his footprints, as they weren't what led authorities to him. He told me, "I never did figure out how the police found me in that house!" He overlooked the simple fact that the stolen car that he used for the heist was parked a mere two blocks away, and they searched abandoned buildings until they found him.

We used to joke about him saying, "One more IQ point and he could be a stop sign!" If he hadn't been Caifano's cellmate, he would never have been part of the Grand Avenue Crew, and he and all of us knew it.

Frank Schweihs told me one time on tape, "You see what happened to Marsh, because of that idiot?"

Rodgers testified in the Family Secrets trial that he had committed arson for profit at the request of Anthony Pellicano. One was a house in the suburbs and the other place was a restaurant not far from my place where he had tried to give me $1,500 to do it for him but, naturally, I declined the offer. It seemed that no matter what ideas he came up with, they never seemed to work out the way he planned.

Everyone tired of him and his failed schemes, including his manufacturing of Quaaludes with my equipment. He felt unwanted by the crew which was the contributing factor in his approaching me to be bought out of his part of the take from my place. After the buyout, he relocated to Texas and got involved smuggling drugs in from Mexico.

Hank, my FBI handler, told me that they had arrested Rodgers for his drug trafficking exploits down in Texas. He had gone there to interview him. Rodgers was looking at life in prison, but he still had something to negotiate a deal with: his connection and knowledge about The Grand Avenue Crew.

He went into witness protection and later testified against Caifano on a stolen stock deal and Joey Lombardo on another, separate case. Hank told me what he said during the interview. "You have to talk to this guy named 'Red.' He knows everything about everybody."

Rodgers never knew that Hank was just comparing my notes with his statements. When Hank returned, he called me and told me about the debriefing. We both got a laugh when he said that Rodgers told him, "Ya otta get ahold of that Red guy, he knows everything about everybody!"

Hank and I laughed about the whole exchange for a full five minutes. He told me he really had a hard time keeping a straight face as Rodgers babbled on about this "Red guy." Rodgers was then placed into the Witness Protection Security Program which federal officers term "WITSEC."

Joseph Lombardo Makes a Point and Lives Up to His Nickname

J oseph Lombardo (JL) earned his reputation as "Joey The Clown" for a number of reasons. Well known are the frivolous protests and motions in the courtrooms but lesser-known are some of his exploits and philosophies on how things should be run by the crew. JL had the good sense to try to help everyone learn how to operate so as not to draw too much attention to themselves or their activities. Let me explain what I mean with a true story to help illustrate my point.

Joseph Lombardo (JL) 1980 (Courtesy of John Drummond)

Michael Swiatek was a big, beefy concrete contractor who knew a lot about buildings. He did hard and heavy work. He was also a demolition and explosives expert, a talent that he only used when he was called upon to employ it. Through his various exploits, he bought the flashiest gold-link chain, ever.

It was unlike anything I had ever seen, and Mikey had it custom made to his specifications. The thing was massive and the individual links that joined the necklace were so large that we joked that he could probably have towed a truck with it. It weighed around three pounds and was his pride and joy.

Anyone who got close to him noticed it. People from a good distance could easily make out the shapes and tell that it was an extravagant oddity. It was so over the top that it actually resembled what might be regarded as "cartoon jewelry." I think you get the picture.

Mikey always attracted a lot of reactions when he would strut the streets with that novelty firmly fixed around his neck. It also made him very popular with the ladies, and he frequently got the best looking girls to go out with him. It was hard to overlook the fact that he was a member of the Grand Avenue Crew and must have purchased it with ill-gotten funds. He had it only for a few months, but he got a lot of use out of it.

JL asked him if he could borrow it for a vacation. He told him that he was going down to Miami Beach, Florida, and wanted to use it to help attract and impress the gals.

Mikey was in a real bind because he certainly could not deny the request of his boss. JL fully expected him to comply and accepted the chain without hesitation. Mikey turned pale as he handed it over. I learned that Joey had been waiting for the right opportunity to approach him, and it was time to teach Mikey a lesson.

Joey returned a couple of weeks later, but he never approached Mikey to return the chain. Mikey couldn't build up the nerve to ask him about it directly so he asked other guys to inquire about his chain and when JL was going to return it. This went on for several months.

One weekend evening while Joey was sitting by the pool in a chaise lounge at Jimmy Cozzo's place, Mike finally got up the nerve to ask him what had happened to his chain. Joey reached into his shirt pocket and pulled out a very petite gold necklace that couldn't have been worth more than $80 and handed it to Mike.

Mike looked at it and said, "This is not my chain."

Joey, while leaning back in the chair, puffing on his cigar and blowing smoke rings, said, "Sure it is. Doesn't that look like the same one that you gave me?"

Mike retorted, "No, mine was a lot bigger! Maybe fifty times the size of this one."

That was when Joey said, "I don't know about that salt water. It must have shrunk it."

All of us who were hanging out there burst out laughing, all while Joey kept a very sober face. Needless to say, Mike's chain was never mentioned again.

In his own joking way, he had taught him a lesson: *you don't look like you are better than your boss*—and Joey was the boss. I recall him sitting by the pool in that same chair, blowing smoke rings from his cigar, saying, "I am a shining star, and there is no others!"

Mikey must have forgotten the lecture that we had all heard previous to this, about driving expensive vehicles. At one time, long before the incident with the chain, we all gathered in the same location, at the bequest of JL.

He went off on a rant about how he had to drive around in a ten-year-old beat up, dented Dodge while other people, well beneath him in the echelon, were driving new Cadillacs.

He told everyone, "If I have to drive around in that piece of shit, who the hell do you think you fuckin' guys are that you can own a better car than I can?"

Some of the people hung their heads in shame and disposed of their Cadillacs almost immediately, replacing them with smaller, used cars.

Joey specifically said, at that meeting, "This kid is exempt!" while pointing at me. After all, I was a legitimate businessman and could account for the earnings that paid for my luxury cars while many of the crew's tax statements showed that they were barely scraping by—that is, based on their primary job's earnings.

It also bears mentioning that Joey had only filed taxes for making an income of approximately $36,000 a year. The IRS has long been one of the worst enemies of the Outfit.

Another example of how JL lived up to his nickname happened in November of 1992 when he was released from prison. He took out newspaper ads in the major Chicago area newspapers which stated:

"I am Joe Lombardo. I have been released on parole from Federal prison. I never took a secret oath with guns and daggers, pricked my finger, drew blood or burned paper to join a criminal organization. If anyone hears my name in connection with any criminal activity please notify the FBI, local police and my parole officer, Ron Kumke." He did this in response to the several cover stories which had been in the headlines, because his release was a major news story on both TV and in the papers.

Joey came "Out of the Patch." That phrase referred to a very poor Italian American neighborhood on Chicago's West Side. He started out as a burglar, and his specialty was taking down big businesses and ransacking them, along with his pals Frankie Schweihs and Jimmy Cozzo.

He was a collector of specialty construction equipment and tools that could be used for both legitimate and nefarious ventures. He would loan them out, and in place of rent he would get a piece of the action from each job. This kept him in the know on what was going on and got him acquainted with a lot of powerful people.

He brought up many of his childhood buddies in his Outfit crew: Larry and Joey Pettit, Irv Weiner, Phil Alderisio, the Spilotro brothers, and several others that died along the way. This helped propel him into a position of power and influence that made the more established, older gangsters double down on their positions and try to keep the "Young Turks" out.

I should note that it was reported to me from several of the "Made Guys" I knew that this statement came from Tony Accardo's mouth, himself, in speaking of these Young Turks: "These guys all came from the same place that you did and have the same skills, so why not give them a piece of the pie now? Because they will eventually overtake us and be running the show anyway!"

Mob guys who could think progressively were adaptable and made it through transition times—and those who didn't were eventually murdered or went to prison and died there.

The Last Supper Confiscated at Ceasars' Home

Irwin Weiner and His Contributions to the Outfit

I rwin "Irv" Weiner was a profiteer for the Mob. He was a close childhood friend of Jack Ruby's older brother. Jack Ruby was the man who was famous for gunning down Lee Harvey Oswald, President John F. Kennedy's alleged assassin. He was so well acquainted with Jack that he was even summoned before the Warren Commission for questioning regarding the assassination.

Let me just say that he knew a lot more about the events of those days than the public ever did. It should also be known that Red Dorfman, father of Allen Dorfman, and Jimmy Hoffa were close friends and associates; all of them had immense financial gain from JFK's murder. No one will ever know his role in the death of JFK.

* * *

Irv also came from "The Patch" and was a longtime associate of Joey Lombardo. Because of his Jewish ethnicity, he was never able to become a full-fledged "Made" boss, but that formal title was really all that he was missing. His influence and authority were immense. He had a great mind and propensity for schemes that resulted in big payouts.

He was licensed as a bail bondsman and used his American Bonding company, Weenie World Corporation, and Danny Seifert's Plastic-Matic Products fiberglass factory to launder money and generate business leads for Outfit interests. His peers also referred to him as "The Rabbi," partly as a reflection of his Jewish heritage but also in homage to his truly gifted intellect.

Early in his career, he controlled the Chicago Outfit's interests in Havana, Cuba. He frequently went to Cuba to oversee their casinos. While there, he also wrote bonds for businessmen such as Jimmy Hoffa and other mob-connected individuals. He was a genuine powerhouse, in every sense of the word.

Irv was a short guy, around 5' 3", but very stocky and well built. Like so many other of the guys in the crew, he had been an amateur boxer in his younger years and had also picked up fighting skills from the street.

His best attribute was making money for the mob. He was extremely creative. He had a close relationship with Felix Alderisio AKA "Milwaukee Phil" but an even closer relationship with Tony "The Ant" Spilotro. They built Circus Circus Casino together out in Las Vegas, with the help of Jimmy Hoffa's Teamsters Pension Fund Loan. They skimmed as much as they could from it and shared it with the rest of the Grand Avenue Crew.

I suppose I would say, in my own words, "Ya see, that's how it's done, Chicago Style."

Irv had a modest home in Niles, Illinois, that he shared with his daughter. At one time he purchased a Boeing 707 to travel back and forth from Las Vegas to Chicago or Deming, New Mexico. The Teamsters had a factory in Deming where they manufactured model trucks that they would send out to the local union chapters. The local unions would have to buy the models, at top price.

When Irv got hold of the plant, they also molded five-gallon plastic pails. A lot of money was laundering from the Teamsters Pension Fund through the plant in Deming, and in his own way, Irv Weiner was a genius. Like most Mob bosses, I often wondered what they could have accomplished if they had set their minds to legitimate business. Many of them were born into the slums and never had a chance for a lot of formal education, but I am confident they could have done very well for themselves if they would have wanted to pursue advanced degrees at the university level.

STOLEN WESTINGHOUSE STOCK

Marshall Caifano had been working with Johnny Rodgers on some counterfeit stock certificates. The real ones were stolen from Chicago's O'Hare Airport. Their value was a whopping $3,000,000. Marshall asked me to go to my bank and take out a loan for as much as I could, using the Westinghouse Stock as collateral. He said, "They will never refuse you, a straight business man, but someone, like me, would never get the loan—and I'm still on parole." I called my FBI handler, Hank, and told him about it. I assumed he made the report. I put off Marshall and didn't go along with his plan for me.

Marshall Caifano, West Palm Beach Mugshot

Later, in 1979, Caifano went to a financial institution in Miami and the banker who made him the loan called the FBI and told them that the stolen stocks were there—the genuine articles. Marshall was arrested and held in West Palm Beach. He wrote me a letter, telling me how we could still do business through his nephew, an attorney. By the time the letter got to me, Joey Lombardo sent Phil Amato to pick up the $250 per week that I was still paying in street tax.

After a few weeks of collections, Phil told me Joey was asking about the factory. I told him that Rodgers took it over, and Marshall had told him to cut me out of the business. JL and Phil wanted to know where the RUSH, and Dr. Popper manufacturing equipment went, so Phil and I headed to the warehouse together.

We opened the doors, and all the equipment was gone! The place was completely empty. Rodgers had sold everything for seed money in order to try his hand at importing drugs from Mexico. I suppose he figured that was an easier way to make money than by direct manufacture of drugs.

I gently reminded Phil that Johnny had ordered me that this was no longer my factory or equipment and that Marshall had told me to stay away from it, so I did as I was told. When Joey heard back from Phil, he was unhappy about it but not angry at me.

Using information from Johnny Rodgers' statements as he became a protected governmental witness, Caifano was convicted in 1979 and sent to Oxford Federal Prison in Wisconsin while JL did some time for his own crimes, relating to Operation Pendorf, where he and Allen Dorfman had been indicted for trying to bribe the U.S. Senator from Nevada, Howard Cannon, and for racketeering.

It was clear to the prosecutors, through their wiretaps, that they had a solid case. While Joey went away to prison, Allen Dorfman's fate was to be gunned down in front of the Lincolnwood Hyatt House when he was out on bond and with his "trusted friend" Irwin Weiner.

Allen had been fortunate enough to show enough income, on his tax returns, to be eligible to make bond, unlike JL. It is obvious he would have been much safer if he had just gone to prison, but he simply didn't want to do the time.

Allen had been in prison before and thought it was safer to be out on bond—until he was shot down, allegedly by Frank Schweihs, near the car that he drove to the Lincolnwood Hyatt House Hotel for lunch [with his close friend Irv Weiner]. Irv's statement to the police was that he never saw who did it, because he did what he was told when "someone" told him to turn around and put his hands on the car. The thieving man had said, "Give me your wallets." Irv told authorities he was just doing as he was told and had been in fear of his life during the armed robbery.

This is the way it was done by the Outfit: someone you trust would bring you to a place, and you'd never return from it. You're led to your murder by a close and trusted friend whom you'd never suspect to betray you.

MARK HANSEN SHOOTS HIS BROTHER

After a normal late-night closing of the bar, I set the front door buzzer so that I wouldn't hear it ring, shut off the ringers on the phones, and then crawled into bed. I had only been asleep for about an hour and a half when I was awakened by some pounding on my back door. I had no doorbell on that back door which was of heavy duty, solid wood construction with a pair of dead bolts for added security.

My back door was on the second floor, and I had an elaborate deterrent system in place to keep people out of the backyard/beer garden, so I was shocked to hear anyone pounding on it. I got out of bed and grabbed my pistol and headed to the back. With my .45 in my right hand, I opened the locks with my left and prepared for the worst. I didn't know what to expect.

I then heard, "It's Mark, it's Mark, open the door!" I opened it and saw a frightened Mark Hansen. His curly light brown hair was all over the place, and he was in some dirty work clothes that looked and smelled like he'd come straight from the barn.

Mark was running his own place, Glenwood Stables, by now and was doing quite well for himself. I asked him how he got up to my door. He was frazzled as he kept saying, "I killed my brother, I killed my brother, and I'm going to prison for the rest of my life!"

He was emotionally distraught and disturbed. I pulled him into my kitchen and secured the door. I asked him why he would come to my place. He told me he needed help and wanted to hide out there, that I was the only one he could trust. I put my robe on and asked him to tell me more about what had happened, while we stood in the kitchen together.

He kept repeating his same phrase, "I killed my brother, I killed my brother and I'm going to prison for the rest of my life!" I had to coax more information out of him, as he was still in shock as tears ran down his cheeks.

I asked him how he killed him, and he replied, "I shot him with this!" as he produced a nickel-plated .25 automatic.

I soon became more awake as I laid eyes on the firearm. I removed the pistol out of his hands and put it on the dryer that was next to the door. His lip was still quivering and his hands were still shaking, as we continued our exchange of information. He had to use the bathroom so I told him to get in the shower as I got a robe for him and put his dirty clothes into the washing machine.

While he showered, I went and woke up Lenny. He was none too thrilled with the prospect of helping out with another problem child.

Mark finished showering and put on one of my robes, but it hung on him like a blanket, owing to his small build. His clothes were still in the wash, and we stood in the kitchen while he sat on top of the dryer. He was still upset, but at least now he was clean.

At this point I asked him a few questions, as I was very curious about things. I asked him how he'd gotten into the city and he told me, "I took ma's car."

"You mean her brand new Lincoln?" He confirmed that was the car he drove in, also telling me that he had parked it in the parking lot. I asked him which one and then learned it was Frank Schweihs's.

Frank had a habit of taking a sledgehammer to the car of anyone who used his parking stalls without authorization and then called Lincoln Towing Company to take the vehicle away. Things just seemed to keep getting worse!

As Mark continued babbling on about how he'd killed his brother, I asked, "Where did you shoot him?" He began to tell me his story.

He said that he was trying to call his girlfriend Joanie, and the phone had just kept ringing. He tried it again and again. When it was finally answered, his brother Danny was the one who was on the line.

He told me that he hung up and drove straight to her house, taking his pistol with him. He told me that the reason he'd brought the pistol was to intimidate his brother since he didn't want to get beaten up by him.

When Mark arrived at Joanie's, her parents were on vacation, leaving the house to their daughter. When Mark knocked, she answered but refused to let him into the house. Asserting his masculinity, Mark pushed his way through the door.

The commotion at the door brought Danny to investigate. He emerged from the bedroom, only wearing his underwear, threatening his brother and telling him to get out of there—or he was going to call the police. Mark took the pistol out of his pocket and pointed it at Danny.

As Danny reached for the phone, Mark extended his hand and told him to put the phone down or he would shoot him. Danny looked at him and told him, "You don't have the balls!"

Mark told me, "I did just like you taught me to, Red. I extended my arm as far as I could, held the pistol with both hands, then closed my eyes before I shot!"

It appeared Mark expected me to approve of his shooting techniques that I had taught him while out at the barn. I remembered thinking, tongue in cheek, that this was not how I'd taught him.

While Mark's eyes were closed, Danny held out his hand, and Mark heard him say, "Don't shoot!" When Mark opened his eyes to see the results of his shot, there was blood everywhere and his brother was laying on the floor in the kitchen.

Mark then told me, "I took Joanie and put her in the car and drove straight here, figuring I could hide out here with you."

I asked him where Joanie was now, and he told me that she was waiting in the car. It had been close to an hour by now, and I was wondering if she had left the car and had created a scene in her own right. Putting her on hold in my mind, I asked Mark where he had actually hit Danny with the bullet.

He said, "I don't know because my eyes were shut so I didn't see, but there was blood everywhere. He wasn't moving when I left!"

His clothes were now done with the wash cycle so I moved them into the dryer as we continued. We went into the living room where Lenny was eavesdropping on the entire conversation. I reached for the telephone as I asked Mark what town Joanie lived in. I wanted to know where the nearest hospital was so I could determine where Danny had been taken.

The nearest hospital was South Suburban Hospital so I dialed 411 and got their phone number and made the call. When the gal answered the phone, I asked her to transfer me to the emergency room. After eight or nine rings, a woman answered, and I told her I was checking on the condition of Daniel Hansen. She said, "One moment please." as she put me on hold.

The whole time I was on hold I was thinking that they had put a trace on the call and that the police would answer from there in the emergency room. To my surprise, Danny was the one that answered with a gruff, "Hello." With that, I quickly hung up the phone without saying a word.

I looked at Mark and said, "Well, there's good news and bad news. Your brother is shot, but he's alive."

Mark now changed his mantra to, "I'm going to prison, I'm going to prison, I'm going to prison." His clothes were finally dried by now, and I told him to get them out of the dryer and to get dressed.

While Mark was in the bathroom getting dressed, Lenny looked over at me and said, "This is another one of your fine messes, Red! How do you get me involved in these things?"

In an authoritative voice, I told him, "Just shut up! I'm gonna need your help."

Lenny took a deep breath and said, "Okay."

I told Lenny to turn on the TV to the early morning news, and the same story was on every channel. The news had reported that a young, south-suburban man had shot his brother, kidnapped a young woman, was armed and dangerous and on the run.

Mark exited the bathroom just in time to catch the report as a picture of both he and Joanie flashed on the screen, with their names and ages beneath each photo. He again affirmed that he was going to be going to prison where he would be sexually abused and molested.

I sat Mark down and told him that he was not going to be going to prison if he would listen to me and do exactly as I instructed him. "The first thing you're going to do, now that you're dressed, is go down and get your girlfriend, and bring her back up here."

Mark became more alert as he began to implicitly follow my instructions, even though he was still scared.

As he went out the door to retrieve Joanie, I picked up the phone and called his mother. When she answered the phone, she told me, "I can't talk to you right now. There's a lot of police in the house with a search warrant, looking for guns!" She then hung up.

I began disassembling Mark's pistol, deliberately damaging it as I broke it down into individual pieces. Mark returned to the back door with his girlfriend, and we all sat in the living room.

As I introduced myself and Lenny to her, I asked her if she was okay. I was most concerned about her mental state at the time as I wondered what the circumstances of her kidnapping were. I was afraid that she wouldn't speak to me openly, with Mark there beside her. I instructed Lenny to take Mark for a ride in the car and get some Dunkin Doughnuts, as I needed an excuse to get Mark out of my apartment.

As Lenny began to leave, I handed him the damaged pistol parts, telling him to drop one part in one sewer, another in another sewer, and to make sure they were at least a few blocks apart.

As they left, it was still dark outside. I began to talk to Joanie, now that we were alone. From the news reports, I learned she was eighteen-years-old; she looked very young and innocent.

She was commenting that she was going to be in big trouble when her parents got home from their trip, as they had told her not to have anyone over while they were out of town. She was a slim, attractive young girl with long chestnut hair and a bit taller than Mark, at around 5' 8."

I asked her if she was being held against her will, and she said, "No." She told me that she willingly accompanied Mark into the city.

I told her, "You can leave at any time if you want to. I can call a cab for you or anything you need."

She said, "No, that's ok, I love him. We even made love out in his mom's car right in the parking lot before he came up to see you. I'll wait until Mark gets back before I do anything. I hope he follows your instructions. You seem to be a very smart man."

I was glad she was being so candid with me. I could tell I had her confidence, even if her perspective on those events was vastly different from mine. When Mark and Lenny returned, I told Lenny to go back and get the doughnuts, which he had forgotten in all of his excitement—and to take Joanie with him this time.

I asked Mark for his father's phone number, as I had not been in contact with Kenny for several years. Reluctantly, he gave it to me saying, "Please don't call him, he'll turn me in!"

I called his father, and we had a short conversation. In a cryptic way of speaking, I asked him if he had seen the news yet. He assumed that Mark was with me. He asked to talk to Mark but Mark shook his head as he overheard the conversation.

Ken and I discussed Danny's condition. He told me Danny would be out of the hospital in two days. I told him to do me a favor and have Danny get in touch with me when he could.

He asked me if Mark was okay, in his morbid fashion, telling me, "I told him, if my brother did that to me, I'd be waiting in the weeds with a gun!"

He furthered the conversation with, "We have to get him out of the country." This was Kenny's code for "out of the state." He always used the royal "we" whenever he spoke about himself. He was cool, calm, and collected as he talked things over with me.

The pieces all came together for me as I talked to Kenny, as to why Mark had shot his brother. I said goodbye to Kenny and hung up the phone.

I asked Joanie, as she had returned from the doughnut run, if she had a driver's license and knew how to drive a car. She told me she did. I told her to drive the Lincoln back to Beverly's place, and she agreed.

I told her, "When the police question you, tell them you dropped Mark off on the highway somewhere out in Indiana." She assured me that she'd make it sound convincing. She did exactly as I instructed.

Mark begged me to let him stay in my apartment building. I told him that it was out of the question and that he would do everything precisely as I told him to if he wanted to stay out of prison.

"I will do exactly as you say, Red. I just hope it works!" as the tears continued to roll down his cheeks.

I called a former employee of mine who lived a couple of thousand miles away. I told him that a young man named Mark was going to come out and stay with him and that I would talk to him later. He agreed to let Mark stay with him and then hung up the phone.

I then called the airlines and made a 1:30 p.m. reservation, under my own name, for the flight, as I paid for it on my credit card. I then called up my father and told him to come to my apartment immediately. He said he was on his way, as he hung up the phone.

I told Mark to empty his pockets and his jeans, including his wallet. I took his driver's license and credit cards or anything else that could identify him and put them into an envelope.

Mark had never been on an airplane in his life, much less a jet. He told me he was afraid of flying but not as afraid as he was of going to prison. I put the envelope away. I took $2,500.00 in cash, and gave the cash and Mark's empty wallet to him. I told him that my father would be driving him to the airport.

It also bears mentioning that all throughout our exchanges Mark was clutching a Bible close to his chest, rocking back and forth. He again pleaded with me to stay, but that simply was out of the question and not up for discussion.

When my father arrived, I told him that I wanted him to take Mark to the airport and to pretend that he was his son. Still holding his Bible, Mark now reached up and gave me a big hug as he and my father left. I told Mark to call me when he arrived at his destination and to call me once a week to give me regular updates. I explicitly instructed him to leave the ticket bearing my name in his seat on the plane, as he left.

My dad returned, telling me that the airline had a problem with him getting on the plane since Mark didn't have any ID, but my father's assurance that this was his son, while showing them his own ID, was enough to get him boarded. Mark safely arrived in the new city and called me collect to confirm he was there—and that everything was going as planned.

I GET A NEW ROOMMATE

I called back Mark's mother, Beverly, and she told me that the police had questioned Joanie when she returned the car. Everything had gone as anticipated, and I asked how Danny was making out.

She said that he was okay and then said, "That cunt is with Danny at the hospital right now! I better get used to it. She is going to be my daughter-in-law one way or another, no matter which one she chooses."

Danny later confirmed to me that she went to the hospital prior to his release and performed oral sex on him while he was in the hospital bed. I rolled my eyes when I heard about it.

I talked to Beverly every day. She was worried about Mark. I told her he was safe, and she was better off if she didn't know where he was. She told me that he needed to see Art O'Donnell, their family lawyer.

I replied, "We need to keep him out of this. Just trust me, Bev, he's gonna be okay." Bev trusted me, too, and went along with the plan.

Several days later, Danny called me and asked what I wanted with him. I asked him where he was living. He told me he was living with five or six other guys in an apartment and that he hadn't paid them any rent so they were about to throw him out. He asked me if I knew what his brother had done to him.

I told him I knew all about it. I asked Danny to come and see me. He asked me why.

"Because I am going to make you an offer you can't refuse! I'm going to get you back on your feet like you can't imagine, but we have to talk about it in person."

Danny agreed and showed up at my apartment the next day. I told him I wanted a favor from him, and that in return for this favor, I would bring up back payments on his child support so that he could see his son, bring his truck payment current, and many other things.

He told me he was driving on a revoked driver's license, too. I told him I could handle that for him as well. I told him he could stay at my apartment while he recuperated, for free.

With his arm in a sling, we went down to his truck with a couple of other guys who worked for me, and moved in everything he owned into the other, unoccupied bedroom. Danny couldn't lift much on his own so we put it all in there for him.

After everything was in place in his new bedroom, he returned to the living room. Lenny was tending to my businesses so Danny and I were now alone. He showed me a prescription for Demerol for the pain and Keflex, an antibiotic for the gunshot wound, telling me he only had what they gave him at the hospital, and they needed to be refilled.

He then described the shooting incident with his brother. He took off his arm sling and his shirt, showing me where the bullet had entered his wrist and exited out of the back of his shoulder, jokingly saying, "This is my innie and that's my outie!"

He was very fortunate that the bullet had not hit any bones, but it had severed nerves and tendons. He had lost over two pints of blood, amounting in a big hospital bill, which I also agreed to pay.

Danny told me, "My brother is really a nut case, mentally unstable. I never thought he would shoot me!"

"It coulda been worse!"

After several hours of conversation and replacing his bandages, he was curious why I wanted to do all of these things for him. He asked me why I was involved. His father had told him that I had been a willing lover and Danny had believed him. He was understandably cautious in his approach to me, as I did have homosexually-themed businesses and even lived above a gay bar—where he was now moving in.

I said to Danny, "Here's the deal. I'm gonna take care a yer back child support, pay yer hospital bills, feed and clothe you, make sure you get visitation rights to your son, get you a lawyer to modify those rights so you have joint custody, to which I might add, eventually you're going to get custody of Anthony."

I went on further to tell him, "I'm gonna pay your back truck payments, get you a valid driver's license, take care of all of your medical needs, and life as you now know it will be over! Your problems that you have now are gonna be solved, one way or another."

I sent him over to LaSalle National Bank, where I banked. I had my personal banker set him up with his own account and instructed him to transfer a thousand dollars into it.

Danny was staggered in amazement.

When he returned to my apartment, I reached over and gave him two hundred dollars' cash and said, "This is some walking around money." He looked at me with even more surprise.

We sat down and talked some more to clear the air. I was very blunt and told him, "I'm gonna do all of these things for you, and all I ask in return is you don't show up in court to testify against your brother." There was a long moment of silence, but Danny finally agreed to my terms.

Danny was very relieved when the girl that I was seeing at the time stayed the night with me. In the months that followed, all of the things I had promised him were fulfilled. His wounds had healed up completely, and things were going well for him.

He confided in me that all of the things his father had told him about me were lies. He cursed his father for being so manipulative and for his sexual perversions. He told me that his father had always hit on any of his friends who came to visit. He had left school in order to get away from the rumors and terrible things that were said of his family life.

He put his drug and alcohol abuse behind him and now referred to himself as a "recovering alcoholic." He worked with me as an employee on my payroll as he helped with the construction of my new third floor apartment next door to my bar.

He had gone from a bum to an upstanding citizen within approximately one year's time. He now had a real future. He had regular visitation rights restored with his son as he was now gainfully employed and current on his child support payments. He would now show up in court in a suit and tie and was closer to getting full custody of his son, Anthony. He was dating a nice young lady named Patricia, and they decided to move into their own place together and later got married.

THE PRODIGAL SON RETURNS

It had been about eighteen months since the shooting. It was time for Mark to return home. The next time he called me, I told him to get on a plane and meet me at my apartment, that I would have someone meet him at the airport. To my surprise, he showed up a couple days later, at about 9:00 at night with his former wife, Doreen. I had wanted to explain the details of how he would surrender himself to authorities but when he arrived with Doreen, he said he wouldn't be staying the night.

Since he wasn't planning on staying the night at my place, I asked if he was going to Doreen's. He again surprised me by telling me he planned on staying out at Glenwood Stables, his own place that his mother and father had been tending to in his absence.

I only had a couple of hours for him so I told him the drill. I told him that Julius Kole would be the attorney who would represent him and that he would pick him up the following morning to drive him into town to surrender himself to the police. He would arrive at the police station that had issued his warrant, that presided over the town where the crime had been committed.

Mark was scared about what would happen. I reassured him that his lawyer would be with him the whole time so that there would be no chance for the police to abuse him.

Everything went precisely as planned. Julius came to my home and told me that everything went okay. Mark was out on bond for a meager $300.00, owing to the fact that he had surrendered himself. The court date was set, and Julius plea bargained a deal.

The deal was this: Mark would plead guilty to a UUW [Unlawful Use of a Weapon] in exchange for one year's misdemeanor supervision, at which time and upon completion of his supervision, his record would be expunged. Through a comedy of errors on the part of the prosecuting State's Attorney, Danny was subpoenaed to appear in court at the sentencing hearing of his brother. At the hearing, Danny said that he had no malice towards his brother and that Mark needed help.

Again, all went as planned—or so I thought. There was one small matter left: Mark still owed me the $2,500 I had given him before he took flight plus the attorney's fees for Julius.

Mark kept telling me that he didn't have the money. After ducking my phone calls for nearly two months, all so he wouldn't have to pay me, I sent somebody out to see him at his Glenwood Stables.

The man that I sent told me what happened.

"When he saw me, he ran into the house. I thought he was locking himself in!"

Mark came back out and handed the man money, all in $100 bills, and paid off his debt to me in full. He obviously did have the money.

THE COMPETITION

Steve Toushin wanted in on his partners' share of The Savage Theater in San Francisco, but they wouldn't give it to him. Toushin was in a legal battle with Jeff Begun and Paul Gonsky which ended when Frank told me about Paul Gonsky: "I had to whack the mutt in my parking lot and that ended the lawsuit."

He later went on to say, "I put one in his leg to down him and seven in his head, then went into my house and melted the barrel of the gun and climbed into a hot tub, soaking any gunpowder residue off my hands while drinking a glass of Stollie [vodka]."

He was cool, calm, and collected as he described how he murdered Gonsky in the fall of 1976. It was a typical Frank Schweihs operation.

Later, a Chicago Police Detective confirmed the story to me, and the FBI later authenticated all of the details that they could. For some reason, Steve was never charged with conspiracy to commit murder or with murder itself.

The Over 21 Book Store right next door to me, and the Bijou Theatre began to sell pornographic VHS videos. The Over 21 had a 500% markup, at $79.95 a video. I was underselling them locally but Steve Toushin from the Bijou was selling as a nationwide wholesaler through a mail order catalogue.

My sales were not nearly as lucrative as theirs, and this outlet venture was all my idea. I had opened a motion picture production studio in Los Angeles, producing my own films and wholesaling them, unlike Toushin who ran all operations out of Chicago.

* * *

The Over 21 never paid the Chicago Outfit anything, as they were out of Cleveland, Ohio, owned by Bill Gold and connected to the New York crime families. During the summertime, The Over 21 had air-conditioning units that rained down puddles of water that disrupted my customers as they used my driveway to enter my store. They simply refused to relocate them, despite my repeated protests and petitions for them to move them to their own property.

I used to put a hatchet in the coils of their unit on Friday nights after everyone was closed that could fix them—sending most of their customers my way. Another inconvenience for them was the fact that Steve used to get robbed every week. He tried offering me a large amount of money each week to see that he never got robbed again, as mine was the only place that was only robbed once. That one time was more than enough for me, and I took actions so that it never happened again. Everyone on the street knew it.

By that time, I had closed down my peep show booths and changed over to peddling videos. My profits increased over 100%, even though I was sharing them with a company owned by The Over 21.

Once I had the money to buy my own machines at MCI Video out of Kansas City, I had them installed in my store. I was upset that they had installed eight-channel video players in my store, in contrast to the sixteen-channel players they had put in The Over 21 Book Store. The guy who put Paula Lawrence's [Reuben Sturman's mistress] machines in asked me, "What are you going to do, steal our machines?"

I told him, "No, they are there, you're just not going to collect from them ever again."

Every time I did something to interrupt the Over 21's business, they would call their connection in New York. That connection would then call in to Chicago and someone would come over to my place looking for me.

They always made it a point to yell at me in public and threaten me in a very overstated manner. The Over 21 had to pay its New York connections for this service.

It got so bad that the same guy who always came to chew me out told me, in private, "Keep on fuckin them with them. Every time they call me out, I'll split my take with you, giving you $500."

I never took money from him despite the frequent visits he paid me. He smiled at me when no one was looking, as we both knew his outbursts were all part of the act. The arrangement was mutually beneficial to the New York and Chicago bosses, as everyone involved got a piece of the pie.

LOUIE'S PLACE, RICHARD BERNOUSKI AND MY RUN-IN WITH THE LAW

L ouis "The Mooch" Eboli was the son of the New York crime capo, Thomas "Tommy Ryan" Eboli. His father was gunned down in Brooklyn in 1972. Louie had long since relocated to Chicago and was running a racket in street protection and juice loans.

He also headed jukebox and vending machine operations for declared joints. He helped supply me with many of the machines I was using and was a respected man on the streets. The Mooch was part of the Grand Avenue Crew and was acting boss while Joey Lombardo was in prison. He lived in Oakbrook but hung out a lot at his restaurant, the Stone Cottage Pub, in Stone Park, on the West Side of Chicago.

One of his chefs was named Richard Bernouski, who was the owner of an escort service that specialized in prostitution and other vices related to the trade. He wanted to team up with me so that he could fall under my protection. He claimed he was working with Louie, but I knew he was lying, as I was part of the Grand Avenue Crew myself. He was trying to get me to believe that he was a big shot who had even better connections than what I did.

He had been responsible for some problems in my turf, and I put myself in contact with him, via the phone. He spoke to me on the phone, anonymously, on several occasions.

It was common knowledge at that time, to those with real connections, that Marshall had straightened things out with Curt Hansen for me. Richard was trying to intimidate me by referencing Curt as one of his "powerful" associates. It is worth mentioning that Richard was the guy who I had seen Curt beating with a blackjack on the fateful night that Curt had fired me out at the Valley View YAK, nearly a decade earlier.

After he finally identified himself, I told him about his relationship with Curt Hansen and my relationship with Curt, including the fact that I was now with Marshall Caifano—and had nothing to do with Curt anymore. When he asked me to be partners with him, I just kept telling him that we'd talk about it later.

The reason I kept putting him off was because he wanted to meet in the restaurant. At that time, I had an extreme case of agoraphobia: I couldn't walk off the front porch much less go to a restaurant.

Several weeks after we spoke, I received a call from one of his employees, telling me that Richard had been shot. I asked him where he'd been shot and what caliber pistol was used. He told me it was a .32 caliber pistol and that he was hit in the head.

After a moment of silence, I said to him, "Then what you're trying to tell me is that he's dead."

At which pointed he confirmed it with a, "Yes, he is." He told me that, during the police interrogation, he was asked if he had any enemies, and he had given them my name, telling them that I was "mobbed up."

The murder took place on October 26, 1978, at 938 West Wolfrom. It wasn't long after that, Chicago Police Detectives were on my front doorstep with their Chief of Detectives, who we all called Joe D.

After speaking with him for a few moments, he agreed to leave me alone because I had promised I would tell him who had committed the murder within ten days. He knew I was "connected" and had access to resources and information that he could never get.

Looking back, I'm sure that Louie was upset when my name came out as a suspect, because we were members of the same crew. However, he felt about it, he never mentioned it to me. I guess it's best to say that during my personal inquiry the right information fell into the hands of the police's investigation team via a few key phone calls on my part.

Johnny Collini, a business partner of Richard's, was arrested along with William Carr AKA Jevari the Pimp, and Carol Lump, one of his prostitutes and a one-time lover of Richard's. A lot of the story was kept hush-hush because Richard and his associates were into some extreme, sexually-deviant behavior that involved hardcore sadomasochistic acts.

While Collini was arrested, his wife, a tough native Tennessean, came to see me in my office. She told me that if I interfered with the investigation, she would kill me, as she drew a pistol out of her boot. Her fear was that her sister, Bonnie, who was dating a Chicago Police Detective by the name of Dave Paul, would be implicated in the crime. She further told me that Dave Paul disposed of the murder weapon at her request.

It is best to say that when she left me, I reassured her that I would keep everything she'd told me in confidence, aside from her threats—which didn't impress me at all. As a matter of fact, at a later date, I discussed this with Dave Paul himself.

He told me, "What can I do? I was in love with her sister, Bonnie. I was ready to leave my wife for her!"

All of this information was transmitted to my FBI handler, Hank Schmidt. He never did anything about it, telling me, "Murder is not a federal crime; it's a state crime." That's just like he'd told me about the candy heiress, Helen Brach, who disappeared in 1977.

The facts of the case were these: Johnny Collini, fed up with being snubbed his share of insurance collection money from several arsons he'd committed for Richard, hired William Carr, who watched Bernouski's comings and goings from his apartment. He enlisted Carol Lump, a prostitute and daughter of a Chicago Police Officer, to fake an illness by bending over and clutching her stomach, hollering and howling in pain. This was all staged for the night of the murder.

When Richard approached her to offer assistance, she took out the gun that Collini had purchased for the murder and shot him in the face— but it only passed through one side of his cheek. She then fired a second shot, hitting him in the arm.

As she struggled to get away from him, Carr screamed from across the street, as he watched, "Shoot him in the head! Shoot him in the head!"

She dropped the pistol. Carr ran across the street, picked up the weapon, and discharged the fatal shot into his brain, making for a very messy crime scene as grey matter and blood pelted the sidewalk.

My name was now cleared. The police had their criminals in custody, and the case was solved—and there were no records linking me with any involvement to the case. That was precisely what I wanted.

I Was No Angel, Either

My life in the Mob was filled with all kinds of indiscretions. I hardly know where to start so let me just describe a few incidents. I have to say that it was a very difficult thing to be known and allied with mobsters—and not commit murder. I had to know how to walk the line with both the Outfit and the Feds. Finding the right balance was not easy, and I did push the envelope on a number of occasions. Here are a few stories that might provide some insight on my time undercover.

Cabrini Green had a well-earned reputation as a hardened inner city slum inside Chicago itself. The area was filled with government housing. Crime of all sorts was always rampant, and it was a very inconvenient three blocks from my store. One winter evening, a resident drug-dealer decided to make some quick and easy money by robbing my store. I had just pulled up and approached the storefront as he was making his getaway—with a gun in one hand and a bag of my money in the other!

Instead of calling the police, I followed him deep into the projects. I was driving my new, 1974 Lincoln Mark IV, which came equipped with a 460-cubic inch engine, as part of all of the available options in their top of the line luxury car.

The robber was clutched down in the back seat of a cab and had given the long-haired, hippie-type cab driver $100.00 to lose me. I stayed right on his tail, though. We went through red lights, stop signs, and the wrong way down a few one-way streets, but this guy was not going to lose me! Finally, I got ahead of them and turned my car sideways into a screeching halt that left them nowhere to run.

The poor cab driver, being young and stupid, thought he was being robbed. He put his hands up in the air and screamed, "Don't shoot!"

I reassured him that he wasn't being robbed, and that all I was after was his passenger. After some confusion, my worker, Lenny, and I went to remove him from the vehicle. As the thief attempted to keep us away by locking each door we approached, we played a strange game of cat and mouse with him running to one locked door after another.

The taxi driver offered me all of the money he had made for that day's work if I would just leave him alone and get the difficult passenger out of his cab. We finally got into the car and extracted him from the back seat. He had a .32 caliber revolver that he was waving at us. Lenny and I each had our pistols drawn on him, too. A lot of insults and obscenities were exchanged throughout the ordeal. When we finally got to him, I disarmed him and put him into the trunk of my Mark IV, with more than a bit of rough handling.

We proceeded to the Chicago Avenue Bridge, several blocks away, near the garbage dumps. I stopped in the middle of the bridge which overlooked the Chicago River. Lenny and I retrieved him from the trunk and held him upside down over the rail, suspending him by his feet. We held him there for a minute and then dropped him about twenty-five feet into the depths below. Unfortunately for him, he landed in a shallow part with his head and arms thoroughly implanted into the silty bottom of the Chicago River. I couldn't leave him in that chemical-filled river.

I should mention that it was common knowledge that the river never froze, despite sub-freezing temperatures, owing to the many chemicals and other pollutants that kept it from forming sections of ice. Lenny and I looked at each other as we saw his legs scissor-kicking in the air, his head buried in the sediment. Not wanting to leave him there to die, I regretfully went down into the water, retrieved him from the silt, and helped him to the shore. I let him find his own way home from there. Lenny and I got back in the car. After a shower and change of clothes, I returned to the store. We never saw him again and were sure he had learned his lesson.

There was another character, a young black male from the projects, who would frequently beckon me to shoot at him. He would approach me from behind and shout, "Draw, Quickdraw!" while he pretended to draw a gun from his pocket.

He really got on my nerves one time so my solution for him was suggested to me by a Chicago Police Captain on the scene. He told me they could take him to the Cook County Jail, without an arrest. With the request of a $100.00 bill, the police officer who transported him in the wagon paid the intake officer $50 of it to put him in population without fingerprinting him or photographing him—or giving him a wrist ID band. On the way to the jail, the driver of the wagon hollered out his window, "Did you see that dog?" as he slammed on his brakes. I could hear the guy tumbling around in the back. Let's just say it made for a very uncomfortable ride for Mr. Quickdraw.

In case you are not aware, it's hard enough to get out of there with bond, let alone if there is no record of your admission. Of course, everyone there said they didn't belong and not many officers paid them any attention. Several years later, I got a call from a black attorney by the name of Cornelius. He asked me if I knew his client. I was honest when I told him that I didn't know his client's name, as I had never heard of him, but I did recall the incident as he described it to me.

I told the attorney, "I'm sorry. I can't help you."

By the way, Cook County Jail is rougher than the State Department of Correction's prison. I knew that he wasn't a happy camper. There were many occasions where ridiculous stuff like this took place.

I always told the perpetrators, "I can't stop you from what you did, but I sure can break you of the habit. Tell your friends! And if you guys have any problem with it, then you should all get together to come at once so I don't have to do it piecemeal. We can get it all cleared up in one single day." People realized that I was a man of my word to all criminals.

Another guy kept causing me grief by robbing my customers as they left my store. I heard people talking about what he was doing and decided to resolve the situation. I went outside and grabbed the guy and into my Mark IV trunk he went.

It was the dead of a rough winter that was well below freezing temperatures, and we took him on a ride out to the garbage dumps. As I drove out across all of the debris, I was concerned about getting a flat tire. Looking back on that night, I was very lucky that I didn't get stranded myself.

When we stopped, we popped him out of the trunk and pulled down his jeans and underwear, down to his ankles. I had some Krazy Glue for each of his hands that we took from the glove box. We emptied one tube into each of his palms and firmly secured each hand to a corresponding butt cheek. After making sure it had enough time to dry in the cold, arid air, we left.

As I looked back at him in the rear view mirror, the thing I remember most was the sight of him trying to walk with his pants around his ankles. He was another unhappy camper!

One thing was sure: he never came back, and everyone in the ghettos knew exactly what had happened to him. My reputation, at that time, was that I was just plain crazy and would do anything to protect my business, home, and customers.

I eventually grew tired of all of the extra drama and hassle of dealing with criminal activities, so I hired David Daruse to police the front of my store. Dave was a former bodybuilder and was well over six feet tall, a trim 180 pounds—and a real imposing force to reckon with. He usually did a great job of taking care of things and that left me free to do my work.

I once got a call while I was at home from one of my store's employees. They told me that some guy, who was later identified as one Donnie Juma Ville, had tried to park in my driveway, blocking the storefront. Dave had asked him to leave. The stranger responded by obstinately locking his car as he got out of it. Dave reacted by punching him several times, really working him over.

The severely beaten guy went back to his car and brought out his Doberman Pincer to attack Dave. Right after it bit him, Dave picked up the dog by the leash and swung it over his head in an airplane spin, releasing the dog into the neighbor's yard as it cleared the ten-foot wall. The guy threatened Dave as he approached him again, saying, "What did you do to my dog?"

Dave responded by knocking the man to the ground as he took hold of the man's foot in his hands, put his own foot on the man's grounded ankle, and then spread his legs open for the multiple kicks that he then proceeded to impart to his groin area. Dave nearly always wore steel-toed boots, so the force of his kicks must have been very impactful, to say the least.

By the time I arrived, Dave was done with beating him. I told him to leave the guy alone. The man was crying and was very emotionally and physically distraught as he approached me. With a voice that I am sure was several octaves higher than normal, he dropped his pants to allow me to assess the damage Dave had dealt. His testicles were the size of grapefruits and were a deep purple hue. He kept repeating, "Look what your boy did to me! Look what he did! I'm gonna sue you!"

I was laughing uncontrollably as he displayed his swollen grapefruits to me, as shamelessly as I had never seen before. I could only respond by advising him to go to the hospital down the street, and told him to have them send me the bill. He took me up on the suggestion, but I learned that they refused him treatment so I am not exactly sure what he did for relief. Needless to say, he never parked there again.

I once had some trouble with the tavern next door—which I had sold on contract to a couple of guys, a doctor, and his homosexual love interest. I was tired of seeing their indecent exposure in the swimming pool and in the beer garden next door. They threw wild parties with numerous and noisy sex partners. I decided to really send them the message, so I took the steel door off of the hinges that separated our properties. I figured that would curtail them from their activities, as everything they did would now be in plain sight.

The very next day, they put up a privacy fence over the newly vacant doorway. Their efforts did not go unnoticed. I made my way to the place and summoned one of my employees to get me a 30-pound sledgehammer. I took one hefty swing after another and began knocking out concrete blocks in their new wall.

When they called the police, the police just laughed and said, "It's his wall so he can do what he wants with it!" The public exposure of lewd and lascivious acts stopped abruptly. From that time on, they kept their voices down and the back door that faced my bar, closed.

There were enough incidents that mirror these that I have related that I could literally write a book about them. I am sure you can imagine why I was known as a very unpredictable guy with a temper.

Everyone in the neighborhood talked about my antics. It got so bad that Steve Toushin, the owner of the Bijou Theatre—who was getting robbed at least three times a week—sent over an employee with a paper bag full of money if I could please protect his place, too. I sent the guy back with the bag and all of its contents.

After speaking with the FBI, they told me that if I had accepted the money, then it was a form of extortion. I would have been guilty of taking money in exchange for the offer of protection. I was glad I had enough sense to refuse him.

As time went on, no one tried to rob me, but the Over 21 Book Store and Bijou were regular targets. Thugs from the ghettos saw them as "easy pickins" rather than me.

Maybe that's part of why my street tax never increased. That and the fact that I never went to the Outfit with petty problems.

A side benefit of my actions was the fact that word would get back to the mobsters in the area. They knew I could take care of myself and my areas of responsibility. They always got a kick out of my experiences with the local lowlifes, as they laughed themselves into tears, sometimes out of sheer disbelief. I was very creative in how I dealt out street justice, and people stopped messing around with me and my businesses.

Another side benefit of my efforts was how much safer the entire area became for other businesses. The type of establishments that opened while I was in operation reflected the newer, safer feel of the neighborhood. It made for flourishing real estate values and a general increase in commerce.

Always remembering that the FBI handlers told me never to break any federal laws, I did my best to heed their warnings. I also did what I could to make examples of people so that there would be fewer problems down the road. I guess you could fairly say that I had learned a few lessons from the Mob's way of doing business, too.

DEALING WITH A CORRUPT OFFICER

I got a call from a former employee, Don. He told me that a guy had screwed him out of $2,500. When I asked him about it further, he told me that the guy was a Cook County Deputy Sheriff, who had told him on the phone that he had no intentions of giving him his money back. I had loaned the money to Don, to advertise on several sidewalk benches by bus stops.

We talked about it, and I told him it didn't make any difference if the guy was a cop or not, I'd make him give the money back. I told him to call the guy and get him to come into his office and talk to him there. He was to leave the back door open for me when he arrived and make sure no one else was in the building.

That's just what he did. Several days later, he called me to tell me the guy was ringing the doorbell and that he buzzed him in. I made it to the steel back door that he had left open for me and walked towards his front office, which faced LaSalle Street behind my home on Wells Street.

His office was on the second floor of the complex, and I took the iron staircase. I proceeded through the storerooms, headed for his office, and seated myself on the couch in his office.

I just sat there quietly as I overheard them arguing about the benches. Several times, the fat deputy looked over at me and remarked, "Who's that?"

Each time he asked, Don told him, "You don't wanna know who he is!"

I remained silent.

They continued to argue, the man telling him he would give Don different locations for his advertisements. He offered to put them at other locations rather than the ones they had agreed upon. Don refused his offer and wanted his $2,500 back.

At that point, I said, "I was told that you were some kinda half-assed cop!"

The man said to me, "I am."

"Let's see some ID."

The balding fat man quickly and brashly produced a Cook County bifold. I got up and walked towards him as he was seated across the desk from Don. His ID card was on one side of the bifold and the Cook County Sheriff Deputy badge was on the other. I looked it over and then put it into my front shirt pocket, then asked him, "Are you packin'?"

He answered, "No."

I slapped him in the face, knocking his sunglasses off of him, and then proceeded to pull him up from his seat on the chair. He was a very large man of approximately 5' 8" in height and weighing in at over 300 pounds. I rolled him over to the couch, telling him to keep his arms on the couch and his knees on the carpet.

I began to frisk him, searching for any weapons. His rolls and rolls of fat made this very difficult, but I was sure that he didn't have a piece on his person. The man now started shouting at me, telling me that I was in a lot of trouble. I pulled him back up and pushed him into the chair he was originally seated in. He told me again that I was in a lot of trouble and that I didn't know who he was connected with.

He boasted, "I can have you rubbed out at any time I want! I've got connections!"

I told him, "You'd better make up your mind, pal—you're either a crook or a cop!"

Don just sat back and smiled as he watched the show, never saying a word. The guy told me that I had kidnapped him, had assaulted a police officer and that he would have me killed. I laughingly said to him, "I didn't kidnap you."

He retorted with, "Well, you are holding me against my will!"

I came back at him with, "There's the telephone man, if you wanna use it, just use it. I'm not doing anything against your will."

He immediately picked up the phone receiver off of Don's desk and dialed 911. I only heard one side of the conversation between him and the dispatcher as he said, "I'm a police officer! I've been kidnapped...I don't know what address this is!"

Don and I just looked at each other and grinned. He next said, "Just send help!"

At that point, I exited the building the same way I came in, taking his badge and ID with me. I went home and called Don to ask him what was going on. He said that the deputy was outside of the building with several police officers. Four squad cars had responded to his call, and he was gesturing up into the window where Don was talking to me on his phone.

Don seemed to be a little scared, and then I told him, "How's he gonna prove he's a cop? I have his badge!"

Not long after that the police left, the deputy began ringing the doorbell to Don's office. I told Don not to answer it.

That afternoon I called a police officer friend of mine and gave him the badge number and name, as it appeared on the ID I had taken into my possession. He told me that he was assigned to the Skokie Courthouse as a bailiff. I asked him who his sponsor was, and he gave me the name of a Jewish alderman in the northwest side of Chicago.

The next day I called the alderman's office and spoke to his secretary, trying to make an appointment. She asked me a lot of questions like what my address was and if I lived in his district. I gave her my legitimate name and asked if I could see the alderman. She asked what it was in regard to, and I told her that I would only discuss that with the alderman. After putting me on hold for a few minutes, she came back on the line and set an appointment for me for the following day.

I went to see the alderman, giving my name to the secretary as I walked in, to which she said, "He's expecting you. Go right in."

* * *

I went into his office, and we shook hands. As he sat down behind his desk, I sat down in the chair in front of him. He said, "What can I do for you?"

Without saying anything, I flipped the badge and ID onto his desk and said, "It's not what you can do for me, it's what I can do for you. I don't know why you put this guy on the job. Aside from threatening to kill me, he's been conning people out of thousands of dollars, using his badge to intimidate them. He must be an embarrassment to you."

The alderman thanked me for my visit and told me that the deputy was on sick leave at the moment, but it is common knowledge that an officer of the court can't go to work without their badge. I left the office and returned home.

Once I got back to my place, I called Don. Don told me that the guy had come over and returned the $2,500. Don and I joked as I said, "We shoulda charged him juice!"

I later learned that the deputy had lost his job as a result of his poor decisions and my visit to the alderman. Neither Don nor I ever heard from him again.

YET ANOTHER CHANGE IN PLANS

Lombardo was convicted in the Operation Pendorf Scandal and just before he went away, in the early 1980s, he had a meeting with his crew, including me. As I had mentioned previously, he told Frank Schweihs to take care of me and help me in any way he could.

Joey Lombardo, 2006 Mugshot

I had talked to Tom Knight, an Assistant U.S. Attorney, at the Holiday Inn at the corner of Madison and Halsted, along with Hank Schmidt, my then-handler. I told him, "I wanna get out of the business and take down the biggest guy I can when I leave."

I chose Frank Schweihs.

Tom told me it could never be done because he didn't use a home phone and only used pay phones for his conversations. When he met with Wayne Bock, one of his partners in crime, they would meet on a construction site with loud machinery, speaking to each other with hands covering their mouths so that their lips couldn't be read. The Feds couldn't even hear his exchanges with a parabellum microphone. Frank was also a master at disposing of any evidence that could connect him to any of his many crimes. He was even referred to as being "The Babe Ruth" among hitmen by the FBI, owing to Frank's success at murdering people.

"Trust me, he's gonna talk to me," I said. "I've known him for about twenty years now. He trusts me, and Joey told him to take care of me when he went to prison."

After several hours of conversation, Hank Schmidt told me that this was something I didn't want to do. Tom Knight told me that it was something he didn't think I could do. It was something that I knew I could do because of the aforementioned relationships and our experiences together. At that time, they agreed to give it a try.

I was reassigned to Special Agent Scott Jennings as my new handler. Agent Jennings was from the North Side satellite of the FBI, commonly known as "The North RA." Scott was on the Swat Team with Hank Schmidt, rather than the Organized Crime Unit, otherwise known as "The Mob Squad," in contrast to my previous two handlers. He was more of an office agent and looked the part, too.

That may have been what made him such an inept handler of me. Hank had been transferred to the airport, and I honestly think they made a mistake by not keeping me with agents who were used to Mob life and culture. I think this was a major factor in why I had so many problems with Agent Jennings.

Later on, Jennings came by to pay me a visit in my apartment. I schooled him on the background of my operations and plans for the videotaped recordings we would make. He sure was different than Hank. I taught him a lot.

He was also needed to secure the copies of the marked U.S. currency bills that were being used to payout the enforcers that visited me. I had initialed each of them, and we could then reference them for tracking purposes on my own copy machine. After submitting those details and going through due legal process, he secured an electronic surveillance recordings' warrant.

S/A Jennings then came by my place with the necessary audio and video recording equipment. He made an attempt on installing it himself after calling Chicago's FBI headquarters for a technician. I overheard the conversation, and nobody was available to assist so he was told to follow the instructions included in the packaging.

He was not up to the task so I took over. He cleared out to let me get to work while he curiously watched over my installation of the equipment. This was a real contrast to the way the Outfit ran their operations. I was disgusted with the whole situation. It took some trial and error, but I finally got things working. I began videotaping the exchanges with my underworld associates.

Scott Jennings and I very seldom saw eye to eye on different issues. I didn't think we'd get along from the very first time I met him. This proved to be true. One such incident that took place was when Scott tried to talk me into getting Frank Schweihs to violently attack me on camera. When he suggested this to me, I told him, "Why don't you let him hit you!"

He just came back at me with a smirk on his face and said, "It's not part of my job; that's your job, Red."

After the many occasions where Scott had demeaned me with his deceitful lies and self-righteous insults, referencing me personally for not doing things the way he wanted, it got me so angry that I finally called the FBI. Telling them it was an emergency, in the middle of the night, they patched me through to Agent Jennings' home. I told him to meet me at the North RA. When he asked me what was going on, I just told him to meet me there. Paul "Peanuts" Pansko and I packed up all of the electronic equipment that belonged to the FBI, loaded up my car, and headed to the North RA in Arlington Heights.

When we got there, Scott was sitting in his car in his t-shirt, saying, "What's up, Red?" as Paulie unloaded the equipment from my car, putting it into Scott's.

I told Scott, "I can't deal with a liar and especially you!" With that, I got back into my car—and Paulie and I left.

The next day, Lenny awoke me to inform me that Jim Bogner, Scott's boss and the Special Agent in Charge of the North RA, was on the phone for me. Bogner began to chastise me.

In my anger I said, "There is no way that I am working with that liar and asshole!" I told him that he had just lied to me too many times and that I just had enough of him. "None of the guys from downtown ever treated me like this. All bets are off!" Right in the middle of his response, I cut him off by hanging up the phone.

Later that day, I got a call from Hank Schmidt. He asked me what I was doing and then told me, "What do I gotta do, come down there and kick your ass? You guys better learn to get along, or I'm gonna hafta come and see ya." Hank hung up in frustration.

The following day, Jim Bogner called me, saying, "We have to resolve our differences." I agreed to meet with him and Agent Jennings at my home.

Sometime later that same week, Bogner and Jennings slipped in the back way with the very surveillance equipment I had returned to them. I again told Scott right to his face that he was a liar and that I couldn't trust him. Scott, with his typical smirk on his face, said, "Oh, come on Red, when did I ever lie to you?"

I began rattling off numerous occasions with him interrupting me, emphatically denying each one of the examples. By now I was screaming at him, and Jim Bogner was telling me to calm down.

I eventually relented and reinstalled the equipment. Bogner was amazed at my knowledge of the technology and my ability to install the equipment. He made complimentary comments about it in a very obvious effort to smooth things over between us, all the while with Scott watching me do all of the work.

I even had to remark that the Mob treated me better than they did—and that was a fact. That statement seemed to make Bogner more sympathetic to my frustrations with Jennings. I agreed to continue on with the investigation, and they left.

Scott stopped by a few weeks later with the audio and video recorders. I proceeded to install them back into my apartment. As the operation progressed I moved the camera and microphone to where they worked for the best picture and audio signals. Scott had insisted that he put a backup Niagra recorder in the chair where Frank or Daddino would sit. I had a close call with it once, as Frank leaned back and knocked the microphone free and into plain view. I quickly distracted him by pointing to what appeared to be a pistol on my coffee table. In reality, it was a cigarette lighter, but he told me, "You should never leave a piece out like that, Red!" as I showed him how it worked. He chuckled and then got up to use my bathroom. While Lenny drew his gun to cover him, I yanked the microphone wires free and tossed them under the chair. Frank returned to his seat, none the wiser.

I recorded the conversations between myself and my underworld acquaintances and the payoffs for their protection. I had many stressful experiences during those recordings where I was nearly discovered for what I was but we got what we needed. The Feds have gotten a lot of mileage from my tapes.

A BIT OF HISTORY ABOUT
FRANK SCHWEIHS

Now this guy was one real piece of work. I first met him at American Bonding at 1010 S State Street way back in 1970. That place was right across from the Chicago Police Headquarters, at 11th and State. The American Bonding building itself was connected to a restaurant called "Mr. Pats." I was with Curt Hansen, my original Outfit acquaintance, at the time. Among the people that hung out and had an office there were Joey Lombardo, Irwin Weiner, and most of the Grand Avenue Crew. Tony Spilotro was out west in Las Vegas, with his brother, Michael, and the rest of his crew. Frank didn't have a crew because he didn't need one, with the exception of an occasional burglary crew that he would briefly assemble as jobs required, but they were in Hollywood, Florida. Frank did have a number of jobs he did with Wayne Bock, a former football center for the Chicago Cardinals which later became the St. Louis Cardinals.

Frank would also sometimes have a crime boss call him at his home on the beach in Hollywood, Florida, to solicit his help. Whatever problem they had would get resolved once Frank got involved. That usually meant that the person at the center of things would end up dead or disappear, never to be seen again. It was a simple matter: Frank murdered anyone, and I do mean anyone, he was told to—or had asked permission from the Chicago bosses to take out, if the hit happened to be of his own volition. He literally was the hitman that other hitmen feared.

One thing that I know from my time in dealing with underworld criminals is that you never ask them how they got involved with the profession. Many of the Mafiosos were born into crime families with long-standing traditions of disregarding the law while other people had a knack for running with the wrong type of crowds and ended up there because they were very talented in some area that the Outfit could exploit. Frank fell into the latter categorization. He was an excellent burglar and highly-skilled alleged assassin. I say that because he must have been because he never got caught.

As I heard it from one of his associates, Frank began pulling off burglaries and jewelry heists at a very young age. In his very early twenties, he and another thief were chased by some street cops. Frank had a gun and fired at the pursuers, letting them know that he was not messing around. He was unafraid of the consequences if anyone apprehended him while he tried to use lethal force against an officer. Most experts will concur that you don't develop an attitude like that overnight. It is safe to assume he had many unsavory experiences with the law prior to that night's volley of bullets.

Frank followed the path that so many of his criminal colleagues did: any time he was charged with a crime, he appeared before a judge and had this, his first time offense, expunged so that it wouldn't hurt his permanent record as a private citizen. He had repeated that process so many times that I know for a fact that he, the judges, and his lawyers had all become regular associates.

Frank learned to eliminate anyone who would oppose his agenda or get in the way of his pursuits. He had a genuine disrespect towards legal authority figures, and he frequently challenged them any time he came into direct conflict with them. I have spoken to dozens of officers and agents over the years, and anyone who had a run-in with Frank knew that he was a very dangerous man. You had to bring your best game to work with you if you were dealing with him and mean what you were asking if you gave him an order. If not, Frank would exploit your weakness and he would have the advantage—and you could very literally wind up dead.

I had developed a few rules that I followed whenever I dealt with him in order to keep myself safe. I had known him for years and had what could be described as a very favorable working relationship with him. Other people were far less fortunate.

Most of the public don't have any idea regarding all of the murders that Frank was involved in. Let me give you a brief run-down of those that bear mentioning, realizing, of course, that there are many that I am sure I have no knowledge regarding. I am detailing these to you because you need to know more of why this convicted criminal was so feared and respected for what he allegedly did, as he is a major focal point of my own story.

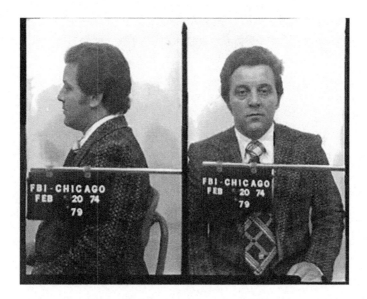

Tony "The Ant" Spilotro Mugshot

In 1962, Frank and Tony "The Ant" Spilotro were connected with the death of Marilyn Monroe, as detailed in the Milo Speriglio book, *Crypt 33*. Frank's then girlfriend, Eugenia Pappas, was reported to have heard of the murder straight from Frank. When his boss, "Milwaukee Phil" Alderisio, heard of his loose lips, Frank was ordered to dispose of her so that there would be no chance of the details leaking to anyone. She was last seen in Frank's car before her body was found the following morning. She was shot in the chest and had unceremoniously been dumped into the Chicago River. Her murder remains an unsolved case for the Chicago Police but only because of a lack of physical evidence. These and other details were outlined in *Crypt 33*.

Anybody that knew Frank knew better than to ever lay a hand on his girlfriend. If they had, there would have been severe retaliation, which never happened. That fact alone lends insight into who the guilty party was. Frank learned early on to keep his mouth shut about any hits he did. He was not one to boast of his work itself—only of his reputation for lethal proficiency. He must have trusted me a great deal to openly share details about the crimes he had committed or planned on committing. He hardly spoke to anyone one at all—much less got personal with them.

Frank Schweihs, Mugshot 1963

Frank has been tied to prominent murders as the alleged assassin of several Outfit members including: the 1973 slaying of fellow Mob enforcer Sam "Mad Sam" DeStefano; the December of 1973 murder of the one-time Chicago area police officer, Richard Cain, who had been on the take for years and was a close personal associate of Sam Giancana and had interrogated Frank regarding the murder of Eugenia Pappas; the 1975 murder of underworld boss and proclaimed consultant for the Mob's side of the Kennedy Assassination, Sam Giancana; the September 1976 murder of Paul Gonsky, a competitor of Pat Riciardi—Schweihs's partner in the Admiral Theatre; the 1976 murder of Johnny Roselli, whose body was found in a 55-gallon fuel drum that washed ashore near Biscayne Bay, Florida; the 1977 murder of hitman Chuckie "The Typewriter" Nicoletti; the January of 1983 killing of Allen Dorfman—the Mob's finance expert that ran the Teamsters Union Pension Fund; the winter of 1985 murder of Charles "Chuckie" English; the summer of 1986 murders of Anthony and Michael Spilotro; and as he had told me on videotape, the 1987 hit on Don Aronow.

Many of these men were trusted personal associates of Frank's, but he was never a man to back down from coordinating or personally performing a difficult hit. Frank could certainly perform orders he was given without a second thought or any hesitation. I was stupefied by how a man could murder so many people without ever being tried or convicted. It was said to me that he was protected by the CIA, after the alleged success in the murder of Marilyn Monroe. One agent told me he was protected by "The Prince on High." I had a hard time speculating on what that meant.

The organization and line of command within the Outfit paralleled a lot of the aspects of the U.S. Armed Forces. Anyone who had a history of actual combat during wartime seemed to merit a higher position within their ranks, right from the start. I know that my training in the Marine Corps certainly opened a lot of doors for me that would have remained closed for other people who lacked the skills and experience that a veteran, like myself, had acquired from their service to our country. Learning to follow orders and respect of the chain of command are essential in mob operations, just as they are in the military.

LOUIE TAKES CHARGE

Phil Amato had been my collector for many years. I had to pay him my street tax after Marshall and Johnny went away to prison. He gave me a farewell message, telling me that "Jeeps" would be replacing him. I had never even heard of Jeeps prior to that exchange, so I called Jimmy Cozzo, Phil Amato's son-in-law, and asked him who Jeeps was. He told me that Joey turned over the day to day business to "That prick out West, Louie." That was how I learned that Louie "The Mooch" Eboli was to be in charge while Joey was away doing his time at the big house.

Anthony "Jeeps" Daddino was one of his street tax collectors, just a mob mule. We got acquainted real soon as Jeeps told me that "my guy" was rounding my street tax up to $1,100 every month. He would be coming to collect it around the first of each month instead of my previous weekly payout. He told me he would give me a call before he came to retrieve it. That way I could have everything ready for him, and he wouldn't have to stay too long or draw undue attention to himself or our visits.

Dealing with Jeeps was always a bit comical for me. He would always take the cash he collected and put it into his sock. Jeeps was afraid to go through the rough parts of town and didn't want to lose it if he got robbed "going through nigger neighborhoods." This statement was documented in court during the Family Secrets trial. Every time I looked at him, it made me chuckle, thinking, "Here he is, a big Mob guy, afraid of getting robbed on the street!"

The Mooch was dying of cancer which Jeeps let that slip in one of our conversations. He was so afraid of his boss that he always maintained that he never once told me that "his guy" was sick, even though it was caught on video tape for the FBI and I to review and replay, which always brought us a laugh.

On one particular occasion when I asked how "his guy" was, he said, "OK."

I told him, "You told me he was dying!"

Jeeps affirmed, in a loud and emotionally charged voice, "I never said that. What are you doing, trying to do get me killed!" The whole exchange was very funny and was a constant sore spot for him.

Jeeps was also very fearful of my Dobermans. He would bring them rawhide chews each time he paid me a visit. I had to lock them up whenever he came over, but that was a common request of any of the crew who visited me.

As I paid him, I told Jeeps to tell his boss to have Frankie get in touch with me, but it never happened—at least not until I stopped paying him. I told Jeeps a dozen times, "Did you give my message to Frank?"

He said "Who?"

"You know who. What's the problem, here?"

"Your guy is bigger than my guy. All I can do is give my guy the message."

What I never knew was that Frank was in charge of everything when Joey was away but he wasn't Italian or a "Made Guy" so Louie was the boss of the Grand Avenue Crew in name only. That was when I stopped giving him the money.

Jeeps told me, "That's not a good idea. Something could happen."

"Like what?"

"You could have a fire or maybe get hurt."

I figured I'd take my chances and stopped paying them.

One day the doorbell rang, and it was Frank Schweihs. I buzzed him in, and as he came up the steps, I said, "Where the fuck have you been? I've been sending messages to you for almost a year now!"

He said, as he laughed, "All I know is I got a call telling me that there was a deadbeat who didn't want to pay his bills."

We talked on camera about a lot of things, even taking over the Bijou Theater, owned by Steve Toushin. We also talked about the eventuality of taking over all of the pornography in the entire country.

Frank told me, "Ya know these walls might have ears." as he looked into the hidden camera. "We have to be careful not to say too much, the 'G' might be listening."

He never knew that I had also recorded Jeeps during conversations about Louie having cancer and dying. He told me to keep on paying Jeeps until Louie died—and then we could make some moves. He had to talk to a few people.

Frank told me, "You know my reputation precedes me, son."

I told him I understood.

Frank left and went back to his residence in Hollywood, Florida, just north of Miami. He told me to keep on giving Jeeps the money until he instructed me differently so that is precisely what I did. I was gratified that he had made it a point to make the trip in to see me, as that was the main purpose for his visit to Chicago.

Louie had a lengthy bout with pancreatic cancer that finally overtook him in 1987. When I heard that "The Mooch" had kicked the bucket, I knew that the time was right for "The German" to seize the opportunity he was expecting. It was soon time for me to seize mine, too.

Frank gave me a phone call, not using his name or identifying himself. He said, "Don't give that guy any more money when he comes around."

I asked him what I should tell him, and he said, "Just tell him you've made other arrangements."

The next time Jeeps called, I told him I had made other arrangements, and he replied, "Okay, buddy!" That was the last I heard from him. No arguments, no complaints. He simply hung up the phone without incident, to my surprise.

I was finally coming to realize just how powerful of a guy Frank was within the Outfit.

FRANKIE IS BACK IN TOWN

Frank discussed things with me as freely and openly as he did with anyone and was always very comfortable. This was likely owed to the fact that I had been a longtime associate. I was always honest in my business dealings, be it a mob venture or a lawful one. If someone in their ranks told me to do something, then I did exactly as I was told. I didn't try skimming off the top or try to cut back deals after a business arrangement had been made.

One time he was telling me about someone he clipped. Afterwards he asked me who I killed. I replied, "Frank, I never talk about my work."

"That's what I like about you kid!" as he laughed with a smile.

All of the guys who I knew that had problems and ended up dead got that way because they didn't abide the unwritten rules of mob-business protocol. My reputation for honesty was a major factor in why mobsters and lawmen took me at my word and advised others to do the same. Frank would never have dealt with others the way that he dealt with me. I was not one to take that for granted. I knew that was going to have to be my way to get to him if he was ever going to be brought to justice.

The guys called Frankie as a joke "Hitler," mostly owing to his German ethnicity, but nobody ever called him that to his face. Because he sat with me day after day, Billy Kent, even advised me, "Be careful—that guy has killed more people than AIDS!"

Even the other Outfit hitmen told their families that if they saw Frank coming, then they were to immediately call the police for assistance. All of that said, he was never rude to me or gave me any problems whatsoever.

As a matter of fact, I had a hard time trying to keep him from solving my problems in his own way, without telling me. Let me tell you part of the reason why. When Joey went to prison in 1982, he called a meeting, and all of his subordinates were there. He told everyone what to do when he was gone. One of the many things he said at that meeting was, "Frank, you take care of that kid [as he pointed to me]. I don't want him to have any problems while I'm gone."

For Joey to tell Frank to take care of someone was not normal—unless it was to murder them! Frank simply nodded his head and said, "I understand."

I have already mentioned that exchange, but it was such a big deal and surprise to me that I think it bears repeating.

After all, Frank did a few things for several of the New York Mob families too, on his own or in his spare time, so to speak. Joey was the street boss, and Frank clearly took his orders from him. The result of Joey's request was a given. Whenever I reached out for Frank through my connections and told him that I wanted to see him, he flew back into town or drove over to make a special house visit. That was the kind of respect and loyalty that was typical of the Mob in those years. Something that Frank, and several others of the old guard, prided themselves in.

Despite my obvious disapproval of the many crimes they committed, I have to commend some of the guys for knowing how to take orders and show loyalty to their ranking officers.

Frank Schweihs came back into town for Louie's funeral and to take care of some of his own business. He paid me a visit and told me, "I don't come out of the woodwork for just anybody."

That's when he explained to me that Joey left Louie in charge of the day-to-day business, but he was the real boss. Louie was just his partner, sending his cut of the money to Florida. He also told me he would be sending another guy around to make the pick-ups. I asked him what happened to Jeeps, and he laughingly said, "I think he's going to open up a hot dog stand in Alaska."

"Frank, I don't trust anyone anymore, either they are in prison like Marsh, or they are dead. I don't want to meet any new people and end up in prison. I don't trust anyone anymore."

Frank said, "Do you trust me?"

"Sure, Frank, I trust you."

He countered, "Then give the money to me, no problem."

So that's what happened. I began to give the protection money directly to Frank.

He looked at me, right in front of the hidden camera while we had this exchange.

"You can give me the money from now on, and we can open things up and take over a few things here, you know, make some moves." Frank continued, "Tell me whatcha know about this broad on the corner." He was referring to Steve Toushin, the owner of the Bijou Theater.

"Well I can tell you this, Frank: I broke into his safe and looked at his books. He's takin' in about a million a month." I referred to my recent intelligence gathering operation. I have a few skills of my own that I used as occasions required.

Frank was very surprised at the amount of money that I told him was in his books. In a very serious tone, he said, "Are you shittin me, Red?" as if I was kidding him. He also asked me if I took any cash from the safe.

He reiterated, "Now that was your idea to do the mail order bit, and he stole it from you, right?"

"Yea, Frank that was my idea."

"And he's with Pat. Pat [Riciardi] was running the Admiral Theater on Lawrence Avenue, was supposed to be turning that money in, and we never saw a dime from the mail-order end of the business!"

He confirmed things again, "You're sure you're right, Red? I don't wanna make any mistakes when I go in with this. That this was your idea, I don't wanna go in and make a fool outta myself when I gotta go see somebody about it."

I retorted to Frank's taunting with some foul language, telling him that it was always my idea, it was my dream, and that guy had moved in on me and had too much money backing him up.

Frank mumbled, "Pat's been rat-holing that money, all this time."

That's when Frank told me, "*I* own the Admiral Theater and the Newberry Theater, too! I built it. Okay, I tell ya what we're gonna do: I gotta go see this guy [Toushin]. I gotta grab him off the street. I gotta make sure that nobody else is around when it happens. What I'm gonna do is ask him for..." He then wrote a dollar figure of $1,000,000 on a paper plate and showed it to me, "and that is what I'm gonna ask him for!"

I looked at the figure on the paper plate and said, "Don't ya think that's too much?"

Disgusted with my comment, he said, "What do ya think I should ask him for?"

I said, "I thought about $10 grand."

Frank got so upset with me that he stood up from the chair.

"That's not enough for the three of us to go to the Super Bowl! Are you kiddin' me? Red, you can't even put a fuckin' roof on your building for that! We can always go *lower* with the rent, but we can't go *higher* with the rent."

Frank was referring to the extortion money he was going to try and collect, speaking in his jargon. This was so familiar to me that I knew what he meant.

Frank was really frustrated with me. "If she's only got $500 grand, then we'll take it. We can always go back for the rest in a couple of weeks. We gotta give her some time. She may not have that much cash lying around [referring to Steven Toushin]." Frank was very frustrated that I looked like I didn't understand what he was saying. He didn't know that it was part of my act.

I acted confused in an attempt to have him say the dollar amount out loud, for my videotape, but Frank didn't fall for it. Frank, finally fed up with my apparent ineptitude, shouted, "Lenny, take him for a walk in the park and explain it to him!" laughing as he mocked me for my lack of understanding of something so clear.

Frank next asked me if I had business interruption insurance because there might be some debris or bricks or stuff that might fly over and hit my building. "Of course, you gotta be outta town if that happens, and then we'll just take the building on the corner." [Referring to the mail order business that Toushin had expanded to the corner building.]

Frankie said, "This is our deal. We kick up to the bosses their share, but you, me, and Lenny are each gettin' thirds. That should be about $300,000 each…that should be a good start."

We talked some more, and he told me he had to go see Pat [Riciardi].

I also knew that if Lenny and I went along with his plan, then it was just a matter of time before we would become expendable. That was simply how Frank worked when his greed and the right opportunity aligned themselves.

Three days later, Pat was found in the trunk of a stolen car. When I asked Frank about it, he told me, "Red, I put him in the trunk of a smoker, for rat-holin'! Don't ya understand?"

I reported these facts to the FBI. I had attempted to report it before it happened, but S/A Jennings wasn't in when I called in the details, so they never got word in time to do anything to prevent it. After it happened, Jennings wrote up an FBI 302 report saying that CI___ Frank murdered

Patsy Riciardi and he, "put him in the trunk of a smoker." It seemed to me that nobody cared.

Later on, in a news story, I learned that Pat got a phone call. After hanging up the receiver, he took off his wristwatch, diamond rings, and a large gold-chain necklace. He laid them on his desk, never telling anyone where he was going. He was never seen or heard from until they found him dead in a parking lot, in the trunk of the car.

With Pat dead, Frank put somebody else in to run the Admiral Theater, a man named Gerald Hector [Jerry] Scarpelli. I'm quite sure Scarpelli kicked in his end of the take up to Frank. Frank didn't have that much interest in the Admiral since his real focus was then on the Bijou's very lucrative mail order business.

During his regular collection visits, I paid him $1,100 a month, as I did Jeeps, all while I recorded the exchanges on video and audio tape. As a matter of fact, all of our conversations for that time period were recorded.

Sometime after Pat's death, Frank told me, "There's too much money in this business. We're gonna take over the whole country. And don't forget, you're my partners. You, me, and Lenny are partners on the whole thing." Shortly after telling us of these plans, he left.

Several days later, Lenny and I saw him in The Crate & Barrel which was directly across from the Bijou, sitting in a chair while monitoring the times Steve Toushin came and went, all in an effort to document his daily business routines. Finally, the manager of the store told him he had to leave.

He had been sitting there for several hours, dressed in his usual clothes and a Minnesota Vikings ballcap. We all laughed as he told me about it the next day. The reason we laughed was because I had seen him there myself, and his story was redundant. At the time of these events, Frankie was living with his son, out in DuPage County. He had given me his phone number to reach him, telling me to never call him from my phone but to have Lenny call him from a pay phone down the street. He would then pay us a visit.

Around this time, Scott Jennings came by to pick up the usual tapes, telling me, "This is good stuff!" He had a smile on his face as he mused over the content we were watching on the recordings. "He talks about the murders and never suspects that it's on videotape."

I told Scott, "They all are comfortable about talking to me about most things."

With that, Scott started down the back stairs, kind of making fun of me, telling me, "Red, the next thing you're going to tell me is that you know who shot Kennedy!"

He hesitated, two stairs down the flight, waiting for my response. He stood there, patiently expecting me to reply. He knew I was close to Marshall Caifano and many other prominent mobsters.

I just looked at Scott, thinking, now why would he ask me that question? He never got a response from me so he left without saying anything more.

It took me a while to piece things together, but I now think he was put up to asking me that question by one of his superiors. I believe they were hoping I'd spill my guts to him about information that Outfit guys had leaked to me about their direct involvement in the assassination of our former President. After all, Marshall Caifano was there, in Dallas, on that fateful day in 1963. He had talked to me about the other Outfit guys who were there, too. It's safe to say that they never did tell me anything about the Kennedy Assassination. We will leave it at that for now.

THE DEMISE OF CURT

While I was partnering with Curtis Hansen when we first got our business going, I drove him to the Hines Veterans Administration Hospital in suburban Chicago. He was going to see a friend there who had served with him in the Marine Corps. During the long walk between buildings, we passed by some quadriplegic patients who were fastened to a wall so that they could see what was going on around them and converse with people as they passed them by.

I couldn't help but feel sympathetic for these poor guys as we made our way through the maze of hallways and corridors. They were wearing a canvas-like straight-jacket "bag" that clothed them and were then hung up on hooks that suspended them in the air at eye level, all in an effort to make it possible for them to engage in normal conversation with visitors. They all appeared clean and well-groomed and were particularly grateful for any exchange they could solicit from anyone who would stop and talk to them.

Curt planned on dropping off a carton of Kool cigarettes to his pal. Several of the guys who saw the box asked for a smoke as we passed them. The area of these patients made a real and lasting impression on me. Curt said to me, "That's got to be a living hell, doesn't it, Billy? That would be my worst nightmare!"

I had no idea that places like this even existed, and I didn't respond to his musings. This was a real eye opener for me as I had never seen or heard of anything like it. I was in a bit of shock while I came to terms with how these poor guys fared.

I couldn't help but contrast the instant compassion that I felt for these poor victims of combat, while Curt showed no emotion at all. He only commented about their fates as though he were a distant observer. He was obviously a very calloused guy.

Curt finished his visit and delivery, so we went back to our other business of the day. Little did he know that his worst fear would eventually overtake him.

Sometime before the arrest of Frank Schweihs, I visited Curt in the North Chicago VA Hospital. He had suffered a brain aneurysm that had required surgery and was now under the full time care of the VA. At the time of his surgery, his wife was a woman named Diane. She was in fear for her life for her entire marriage, as Curt was a very domineering, abusive, and vicious person who would brutally retaliate if she ever left him. I wanted to make sure the rumors about his condition were true, before I left Chicago for good.

When he went to the hospital to determine the cause of his health issues, it was discovered that he would need brain surgery if he hoped to make a complete recovery. Diane had called me when she got the news and told me of her concerns since she wasn't sure what she should do. She really wanted to get away from Curt, but she was trapped by her fear of him.

The doctor who was to perform the surgery had never previously done the procedure that Curt now required. She was told the chance of success was about 50/50, but if it didn't work, Curt would never be the same—and would likely never be able to function normally again.

When I learned of those details, I advised Diane to go ahead and approve the surgery since she really didn't have anything to lose. Needless to say, the surgery had not gone well for Curtis, and he was never the same. Diane was able to escape his clutches.

When I surveyed him in that North Chicago VA hospital, I noticed that both of his legs and one of his arms had been amputated. Only one arm remained fastened to the rest of his body. He had suffered from diabetes and poor circulation in his extremities. That, coupled with his lack of motor skills, made it difficult for him to sit up, walk, or do anything on his own. He was fastened to the wall just like the guys we had seen on that fateful day a few years earlier.

His long, white hair was all over the place. He was alive, but his mind was long gone. He couldn't recognize anybody. He could speak, but about the only thing he could say was, "Yeah."

The first thing I asked him was, "Do you recognize me?"

He answered, "Yeah."

I looked around the room and noticed a Christmas card that was a couple of years old. This told me that nobody had come to visit him in quite some time. The nurses didn't pay much attention to us, either, because it seemed Curt was not a patient who was expected to make a recovery.

I saw that he was eating some oatmeal and asked if he liked it. He just said, "Yeah" again. I could tell he was hardly aware of what was going on around him so I told him bye as we parted ways.

As I left the VA hospital and got into my car, I told Lenny, making light of his condition, "Well, we don't have to worry about him anymore, he's out to lunch!"

I have to again state that it was more than coincidence that the living hell that he had seen others go through was now his own fate. Looking back at his comment while we were at Hines VA Hospital, it really was poetic justice for a brutal man like him to end up living his worst nightmare. His life is a tragic example of that fact.

MY OTHER VISIT

I made some time to pay a visit to Kenneth Hansen. He had renamed the stables Camelot, but he, himself, had not changed in any way from his previous demeanor and personality. He was still up to his usual nefarious, criminal activities.

I suppose I could create a list of the things that had come to my attention, but, in all seriousness, it would simply take too long to come up with everything he had done. For the record, let me say that it would include: the alleged abuse and murder of many runaways who had crossed paths with him over the years; several arsons; and direct involvement in the murder of Helen Brach, the candy heiress. That's just to mention crimes that I am aware of which have no statute of limitation. He was a very bad man in every sense of that description.

Kenny was always trying to find ways to swindle others and capitalize on actions that would lead to a profit for himself. He had gotten away with so many crimes over the years that he became emboldened in his efforts. He was constantly trying to get back the properties he had lost to his wife when they separated—and nothing was beneath him if he had a goal he was trying to achieve.

As an illustration of this fact, I can tell you that Kenny had tried to get me to put a very large dosage of LSD into her morning coffee. This was all in an effort to make her just like her brother, Richard.

Beverly's brother had been living in a state mental institution in Dixon, Illinois, because of his severe, dramatic mental episodes and the threat they posed to himself and others. I had learned, with the help of the ATF, that he had, in fact, been poisoned with a toxic level of exposure to the drug.

It made sense to me that Kenny was somehow involved, and it was an easy connection to make because of his request to me. He had arranged the overdose only a few months after he had committed the murders of the three boys back in 1955. Since early 1956 Richard was institutionalized. When I spoke of this to Kenny, he told me, "Insanity runs in her side of the family." He was trying to get me to believe this lie, but I knew Beverly was mentally sound.

In the late 1970s, I had a run in with Kenny that gave him some new insight regarding me. His show barn stalls had seen a lot wear over the years and needed replacement. He found a deal on some rough-cut oak two-by-sixes, two-by-eights, and six-by-sixes that were straight from a mill in Tennessee. He didn't have the funds to buy them and because of the deteriorating condition of the barn, he had very little income.

I had kind of felt sorry for him and Beverly. His boys were also impacted by his financial condition so I reached into my pocket and loaned him $4,500 so that he could purchase the needed materials. It wasn't that much money to me, at the time, so I acted on my sentimentality.

Ken was shocked at my generosity and suggested I buy a piece of his land out front and build a place out there. I agreed. He had his lawyer, Art O'Donnell, draw up an agreement between myself and Beverly. He ordered up a survey to partition the land off from their property. When I saw the survey, it was not what we had agreed upon. He had moved the property line over, for the entrance to the stables, a good forty feet. By this time, the lumber had arrived from Tennessee.

I was disgusted with his deceitfulness and could see that if I continued down this road with him, we would have more problems. I avoided taking his phone calls for several weeks.

Eventually, Beverly Hansen called me, begging me to reconcile with Kenny. She suggested I call him at the barn's pay phone.

I called him, and we argued. As I paced my bedroom floor throughout the conversation with him, I finally decided I'd had enough. All of the frustration that had built up in my dealings with him over the years caused me to scream into the phone saying, "You look like shit, you live in shit, your clothes are shit, everything that comes out of your mouth is shit, and as far as I'm concerned you are shit!" Even as I was saying this, I was saddened as I thought about the good times I would miss building the stalls in the barn with his son, Mark.

Kenneth Hansen, Apartment 1979

At that point, Kenny said, "Willy, Willy, Willy, when are you going to learn? You never get mad at anybody who owes you money because they'll never pay you. You'll never see a dime."

I countered, "Oh yes I will!"

He tried to threaten me, "What do I have to do, call Vic Spilotro?"

I told him, "I don't care who you call." and with that, I hung up the phone.

About an hour later, I drove over to Grand and Ogden to meet with some of the Outfit guys, asking them if personal problems were treated the same way as business. I recounted the conversation between Ken Hansen and myself. Several people offered to buy the loan and put him on juice, taking me at my word. I was told that Vic would have to get permission to get involved and that it would never happen.

I returned home and the next day, I called the stables. Beverly answered the phone and was glad I had called. She gave the phone to Kenny, and he said, "What do you want?"

I told him that I wanted my money.

"We already discussed this," he said.

"Yea, well...so did I!"

I then proceeded to explain my visit to Grand and Ogden.

This upset him. "Who did you talk to?"

I misled him as I replied, "JL."

"You can't be serious! When I look at that man all I see is death in his eyes."

I told him that I sold his loan to a juice collector. He was now going to have to pay ten percent a week "just for the vig" [interest]. He couldn't believe I did this, and I heard the fear in his voice, as I chuckled and told him, "Goodbye."

In the very early hours of the next morning, I heard my dogs barking and went to investigate. There was an envelope with cash in it between my door and screen door. That was the beginning of his regular weekly payouts until he had repaid my loan in full. I never charged him interest; however, he did pick up the tab for the surveyor and the contract to purchase the property. That was good enough for me so I figured we were even.

Kenny now knew more about me than he had at the other times when I had visited him. He knew that I was not going to be manipulated by him. What he did not know was the fact that the whole reason I came out to see him now was to warn him never to try to kill Beverly again. He had already made several failed attempts on her life. I wanted to make it very clear, in his mind, that if she died under any mysterious circumstances, then I would come after him and bring him to justice.

I drove out to the stables. Kenny was outside, over by the corral. Although Beverly still owned the place, Kenny was the one who now ran the operations. He still lived in the bookie apartment up the street from the stables. He was wearing his fancy derby hat that he used to cover his hairpiece. He was just standing there, and I could tell that he still prided himself on the fact that he thought any manual labor was beneath him.

He had once displayed his hands to me, telling me to take a good look at them while saying, "Do you see any dirt underneath these fingernails? I've never worked a day in my life, and I never will!" It was one of his ways of letting me know that he could always get others to do his dirty work.

When Ken saw me approaching him, he greeting me with his old, "Willy, Willy, Willy. What are you up to?"

I spoke to him a bit and asked if he would play me in a game of chess. He reluctantly agreed to it, claiming that I was always too easy to beat.

We made our way over to his apartment and set up the chess board. The first game I played Fools Chess, and I beat him in three or four moves. Astonished at his loss, he quickly set up the chess pieces for another match.

In about half an hour, I beat him again. The third game lasted about four hours, at which time I repeated my victory streak.

Enraged, he flipped over the chessboard, knocking pieces in every direction.

"You were never a better chess player than I was. I always let you beat me, just to see the way you think. Now you know how I think, and you will never beat me again." I simply told him, "If you ever try to kill Beverly, then I will come after you and put you where you belong: behind bars!"

Again, that was my sole purpose in going there to visit him so with that, I turned and left. I never waited for his response. I got back in my car and returned to my home.

I am sad to say that my threat had the opposite effect on Kenny. Once he saw the news about my testifying against Frank, he gathered together his inner circle and showed them newscasts that reported I was in the witness protection program. He made this statement to them and to several other people who knew me, "That's the last time I'll hear from him! That rat!"

Boy was he wrong! Just like Curt and the rest of these buffoons, they underestimated me. Their own misdeeds and crimes would eventually catch up with them.

I Get Outta Town

C hristmas week, at the end of 1987 and the beginning of 1988, I went to a warmer climate and bought a home. I had always told Frankie that I wanted to move to L.A. and run my businesses and production company there since it was so close to everything I was involved in.

Lenny stayed behind, taking care of the day-to-day business. He talked to Frankie a couple of times when I wasn't there but never got it on tape in the apartment. They talked on the street in front of the store, directly below my apartment.

After about two months, I came back and sold all my buildings to John Henderson, an insurance salesman who owned other buildings near my place. When I told Agent Jennings what I did, his supervisor, Jim Bogner, called me and came over to talk to me. I told him I was ready to pull the plug and leave town for good. He sure wasn't happy about it. He wanted me to keep Frankie talking and to continue to capture our exchanges on tape. It got to the point where Bogner, two other agents, and I went over to John Henderson's place across the alley. Bogner showed him his badge and told him we were in a very important investigation.

"Would you consider renting the back of the building to the FBI for a few months?" Bogner asked.

John Henderson was upset, looking at the badge and the other agents, and said, "I have another office in London, England. I'll go there for a while and you can stay in the building. You don't have to pay me any rent."

I went back and forth from Chicago to my new home, leaving Lenny there to make his plans on where to go when we pulled the plug on the whole mess. Lenny said he was going to Hawaii. I was going to stay on the continent in my new home in a warmer state. I kept in contact by phone every day, but Lenny could always reach me on my SkyPager if something surfaced that needed my attention.

On Friday, September 9th, 1988, Jim Bogner, the FBI SAC of the North RA, called me and asked me to come to Chicago. I caught a flight that night and arrived at O'Hare Airport around 1:30 a.m. I took the L train which let me off two blocks from my apartment, above the bookstore. Frankie was under 24-hour FBI surveillance at that point. We made plans for his arrest for Thursday the 15th of September.

The FBI decided that Lenny would call Frankie Schweihs at around 6:00 a.m. from a payphone, as we were all accustomed to do per Frank's insistence. He told him, "Red needs to talk to you right now, face to face."

Frank responded and said, "I'll be right there."

When Lenny came back to the apartment, there were six to eight agents with handheld radios. They were talking to a pilot in a plane that was following Frank as he made his way to my place. The authorities had painted an "X" on his car with special paint which was not visible to the naked eye. They were using it to track his progress. Frank did a quick stop for doughnuts and coffee, but that was his only diversion. I could hear the exchange from radios as agents were looking around the apartment for spots to conceal themselves. It was all going on right before Frank arrived, and the tension was really mounting for all of us.

That was when it hit me: I was dressed in a suit. Frank always saw me in pajamas and a robe. He might suspect something if he saw me dressed that way so I quickly got out of my suit and dug into an upstairs bedroom closet, looking for pajamas, a robe, and some slippers. I hurriedly put them on in my bedroom while two of the agents accompanied me.

They were asking me how my intercom worked from the living room downstairs, to the other unit in my bedroom. I locked the key that activated it so it would stay on and broadcast what was going on downstairs. Two FBI agents looked for a place to hide in a large closet under the staircase. Two others were in the kitchen, towards the back, and two others stayed in the bedroom, listening through the intercom. Everyone was finally in position and ready for Frank's visit.

Scott Jennings waited for Frank to pull up to my home, and I was standing there listening to Jim Bogner's radio with him. I could hear Scott saying, "He circled around the block looking for a parking place and looking for something suspicious." Frank drove on.

He finally parked in a parking lot down the street. He was in a Jeep Cherokee that someone had loaned him. He walked up to my door and rang the buzzer, saying, "It's me."

Someone buzzed him in, and he came up the stairs. All of the FBI agents had found a place to hide by now and were out of sight.

As I greeted Frankie, he said to me, "What's up, Moe?" I told him that I was leaving town for a while, and I just wanted to make sure that he got his money because I didn't know when I'd be coming back.

He looked at me and said, "You mean you made me come all the way down here for that? You know me better than that, Red. If I didn't get it offa ya at the first of the month, I'dda taken it outta my own kick!"

"I just wanted to make sure, Frank."

Frank counted the money and put it in his left-hand shirt pocket. As he left, walking down my stairs, he told me to be safe and have a good trip—never asking me where I was going.

After he had cleared out of the building, all of the agents' radios turned on, and they grouped together into my living room. They were all staring at him through my living room windows as they watched him go down my driveway.

We all listened to the radio communications as he made his way to the Jeep. The next voice I heard on the radio belonged to Scott Jennings as he yelled, "Put your hands on the hood, Frank!"

Scott flashed his ID and a warrant for his arrest.

"Go fuck yourself," Frank replied and refused to comply with the order.

Scott, now in a shaky voice, told him to put his hands on the hood as he drew his Sigsaeur 9mm. Several agents came to assist Scott, and Frank finally complied.

As they searched him for weapons, Frank asked them, "What's this all about?"

They reached into his shirt pocket to recover the marked $100 bills that I had given him. Two other agents handcuffed him and showed him the warrant for his arrest. When he saw that my name was listed as a victim of his crime, he laughed and said, "You're wasting your fuckin' time, I'll be out in five minutes!"

They quickly whisked him into one of their unmarked cars and drove him away. They searched his borrowed Jeep and then had it towed.

Frank Schweihs, 1988 Arrest Mugshot

After they had left, I changed back into my suit. Jim Bogner handcuffed me and walked me downstairs and into my store. From there I told all of my employees and patrons that we were closed and announced that they all needed to leave. They left without saying a word, seeing that I was in handcuffs and had my own escort of agents. I am confident we gave everyone the right impression.

The FBI took my keys and locked up my store and apartment door. They put me in one of their four cars which were parked in my driveway and proceeded to drive me further downtown into the "Loop."

An agent then proceeded to unlock and remove my handcuffs while they drove Lenny and I on to a hotel where Jim Bogner had rented a room for me, under his own name and credit card payment. Jim Bogner told me that I should leave the following morning and return to my new home, out of state. If I needed anything, I should just call for it using room service and just sign for it under Jim's name—but I was not to leave the hotel room.

Lenny went back to the apartment with the agents to help load up my and his belongings for the moving company. Lenny then flew out to Hawaii a few days later while I headed back home.

There are a number of grievances I could list that I had with the FBI, but just one of the MANY stupid things S/A Jennings suggested was finding the very cheapest mover who could be procured for my relocation. He thought that was not something he should have to be bothered with coordinating. I called several different moving companies and contracted "All Points Moving" for the job. They were the cheapest movers I could find and that was all Scott cared about.

Even when the moving van pulled up to move my belongings, after I had left, Tom Knight, the Assistant U.S. Attorney working with us, made the comment, "What bonehead picked this moving company?"

I asked him what was wrong with the company and he told me to turn on the TV to see it for myself on the news—and not to be shocked to see the big letters, from front to rear of the moving van: "We Move to Florida."

Alan Ackerman, who was also Frank's attorney, lived a few houses away and asked Tom about the obvious location of where the truck was headed. Tom looked at him and, with a note of sarcasm, said, "Do you really think we're that stupid?"

Alan convincingly replied, "I guess not."

To add further insult to injury, when the truck arrived at my new home, one of the movers recognized me because he was the relative of a Chicago Police Officer who was on the take from the Mob.

This is just a small sampling of the problems I had with Scott Jennings. I am sure many people would be amused at the stories I could share in another book that focused on it. There are a lot of reasons why I decided on the title of this book and Scott is living proof. I am sure that I would have done much better if I'd have been passed over to another handler who had an organized crime background and understanding that was innate to his duties. Preferably one from their "Mob Squad" downtown.

At that point, I was just happy I was leaving Chicago.

FREE AT LAST

I was glad to be done with my stint as an informant and relieved that things had all gone according to plans that day. After a good night's sleep, I jumped into Lenny's Ford Taurus and drove through some very rough weather, as I made my way to a fresh start and a new beginning outside of Chicago. I passed through the wake of destruction caused by Hurricane Gilbert. The feeder bands from the hurricane had reached all the way to Kentucky, and all communication was lost between the FBI and I.

No cellular service was available, and they got really worried when we lost contact for about eighteen hours. When we last spoke, I was in the car driving. They were particularly worried about me staying in touch. They feared I had been killed when we lost contact. The poor weather was to blame, though, and I got back in touch with them as soon as I could, much to their relief.

When I arrived home, I tuned in to the Chicago television stations. Frankie was all over the news. It was the first time he was being held without bond. The bond hearing lasted two weeks for Schweihs, while "Jeeps" Daddino was released on bond, the next day.

I later spoke with Scott Jennings about the arrest. He told me that it had been a difficult one for him. He told me that he was afraid he was going to have to shoot Frank because he simply wouldn't comply with his orders. It had taken nearly half an hour to cuff him and load him into their car. Throughout the exchange, Frank's language was filled with vulgar profanities and insults regarding FBI agents. Scott was finally able to see what it was like to interact with Frank on a firsthand basis. I hope he found some new respect for me and the positions he had tried to put me in.

When they took him down to the federal building to explain the charges he was facing and interrogate him, he continued to laugh until they showed him a sampling from one of the tapes. At that point Frankie's mood changed, and he instantly demanded to speak to his lawyer. He wasn't laughing anymore, and he was now very much on the defense.

For almost a week, all of the Chicago television stations focused on Frank's bond hearing, including WGN's nationwide cable network.

Scott Jennings did a remarkable job on the witness stand at Frank's hearing. His accuracy, combined with video proof, was very effective in showing how dangerous Frank was. It was a fruitless effort for his attorney, Alan Ackerman, as portions of the video and audio tapes were shown in court. One quoted Frank as saying, "I gotta go outta town, I got a fuckin' hit. I won't see yas for a while."

Magistrate Joan Lefcoe ordered that he be held without bond because he was a danger or a threat to society. This was the very first time in Frank's life that he was not given bond after being arrested—and he had been arrested more times than his age. In the past, he usually made bond. When he was out on bond, those witnesses who were going to testify against him would end up murdered or were never heard from again.

Things were different now, and this time he sat in the Chicago MCC until his trial in October of 1989. Months went by, and the FBI stayed in daily contact with me to make sure I was safe.

Let me share one unusual incident that illustrates their concern over my safety: a man was taking a picture of my house in my new state of residence, and I noticed him. As he sped off, I took down his license plate number along with the make and model of his car.

I called the FBI in Chicago. Half an hour later, they returned my call, telling me that my local police had pulled a guy over, at their request, and it turned out that this man was just a real estate agent. He was simply looking at the houses in my area for his own business purposes and happened to like something about my home, so he had snapped a photo of it. He was scared to death as the local police asked him why he had taken the pictures. I felt sorry for the poor guy, but at that point, it was better to be safe than sorry. Maybe he will read this book and now have a better understanding of what happened and why.

The Trial of Frank "The German" Schweihs

In May of 1989 Jerry Scarpelli, Frank's chosen man to run the Admiral Theater, allegedly committed suicide while being held in the MCC. He was indicted in the summer of 1988 for robbery charges and had agreed to become a government informant. There may have been other trials they planned to use him on or other reasons people have given for his suicide, but I find it hard not to make a connection to Frank's upcoming trial and some unusual circumstances that make his suicide noteworthy.

Word reached me through the U.S. Attorney's Office that Jerry's suicide was suspicious. I never could understand how a guy could commit suicide with a plastic bag over his head, with his hands tied behind his back, alone in the shower. He was in his own cell in maximum security, unlike the others held in a group pod in that facility, awaiting their trials. Was Scarpelli's demise a coincidence? Nobody who worked there was reprimanded or put under investigation regarding the death—and that remains a mystery to this day, as far as I know. Frank just happened to be staying on that same floor when it occurred. Some people speculated that there was a connection between Frank being there and Scarpelli's death.

In October of 1989, Tom Knight, Assistant U.S. Attorney, called me into town to testify at Frank's trial. The trial was set before the Honorable Judge Ann Williams. John Sullivan, the lawyer for Anthony Francis Daddino [AKA Jeeps], filed many motions to sever his trial from his co-defendant, Frank. In his own words, Jeeps said, "I don't want to be tried with a murderer!" As a result of that statement, a murder contract was put out on him—prior to the trial.

The motions were never granted, and his statement was stricken from the record when Alan Ackerman, Frank's attorney, asked that it be removed. Their day in court had finally come.

I told Tom that I would be in town under my own method of arrival and would just show up at the Dirksen Federal Building. When I got to Chicago, I called Tom at his home. We met at his office, the next day. I parked downstairs in a Secret Service parking stall. One of the U.S. Marshals took me up in the elevator to meet with Tom.

Every floor we went to and every room we entered required a key— even the elevator—and in all ways looked to me like it was high security. Tom and I reviewed some of the videotapes, with me explaining to him the things he didn't understand.

He gave me a tour of the courtroom, telling me that it was a ceremonial one that was only to be used for special occasions, as it was bigger in size than typical courtrooms and could accommodate a lot more observers. I objected to walking from the back of the courtroom past all of the spectators. He assured me that I would be secluded in the judge's chambers, awaiting my turn to testify, before I would be ushered into my seat on the witness stand. I had a good idea of how things were going to work now that I had been given the grand tour, so we parted ways. I stayed with Lenny's sister for a few days in anticipation of the trial.

The day the trial began arrived—and it was nothing like Tom had described. I was escorted upstairs by several agents of the FBI and asked to wait in a small, cold room without windows. It was formally called a "witness room" and was a major contrast from the judge's chambers that Tom had shown me. It was strategically positioned across the hall from the courtroom. I didn't like being confined there.

The temperature seemed to be around 55 degrees. The seats were stackable, fiberglass chairs that didn't lend themselves for a comfortable, extended stay. Rather than confine myself to such an unaccommodating place, I paced the hallways with an agent escort.

In my travels through the hallways, I eventually walked closer to the courtroom door. Something caught my eye. There was a lady who was about forty feet down the hallway, hollering at me to get my attention. She was wearing a woolen, tweed coat and a babushka that covered her head. About five FBI agents locked arms to block her from approaching me. Jim Bogner was with me when it all happened, and I asked him who she was. He told me that I didn't need to know.

I later found out that the woman was Diane Pappas, the sister of one of Frank's many alleged murder victims, Eugenia "Becca" Pappas. Back in 1962 a young Eugenia just happened to be a girlfriend he had confided in, regarding his recent high-profile, murder of Marilyn Monroe. Felix Alderisio [AKA Milwaukee Phil] found out about Frank's recounting of details regarding the job to her, and he ordered Frank to make sure she kept silent.

She was last seen in his car. Her body was later pulled from the Chicago River, featuring a fatal gunshot wound right to the chest. After the incident, Frank had immediately disposed of his car in a local junkyard. They took the vehicle to the on-site, car-compactor—and it crushed the automobile to bits. It left no evidence behind, and all that remained of it was nothing more than a pile of scrap metal. Richard Cain, Chief of Detectives, Homicide Division, interrogated Schweihs about the murder and then released him.

Just like Al Capone, Frank was never tried for murder even though he, too, was allegedly a remorseless killer. I never got a chance to hear what Diane wanted to tell me. To this day, I resent that I was purposely kept from communicating with her by my FBI escort on the day of Frank's trial.

It bears mentioning that as part of Alan Ackerman's opening statement, he confirmed, as a fact, that Frank had offended all of God's creatures in one way or another...but advised juror's not to hold it against him. On videotapes, Frank referred to Jews as "Heebs" and was represented by one in Alan Ackerman himself. He also made several references about "niggers." Judge Williams was African American, along with several jurors, and there were possibly a few Jewish jurors. I'm sure Alan did so because he was preparing everyone for the explicit, violent, and foul language that Frank used in the recorded conversations. That was probably a good judgment call on his part, but I don't think it made much of a difference to anyone by the time the trial had unfolded.

I was taken into the courtroom door and walked down the long aisle, passing the many spectators which included Frank's daughter, Nora, and son, James, on my way to the witness stand where I was sworn in.

This was my first time ever testifying in a courtroom on a criminal case, and I really didn't know what to expect. Tom Knight had simply advised me to, "Relax and be truthful. Everything is going to be fine."

Frank was there, too, under U.S. Marshall's security. Even though he was an aged man, nobody was taking any chances with Frank. I thought it fitting that they took that approach with him, and I was sure that he was very uncomfortable in every possible way.

Tom began his direct questioning. He asked me my name and then asked me if I had owned the business called Chicago's Old Town Video.

I confirmed my name and answered, "Yes," to having owned the business. He then asked me if I was familiar with the defendant, Frank Schweihs.

As he stood, Tom asked me to point him out to the jury. I pointed to Frank and said, "Yes, that's him over there." He repeated the same questions for Daddino.

The next question was, "How long have you been an FBI informant?"

"Since August of 1971."

"As an informant, did you receive money from the FBI?"

"Yes I did."

"How much did you receive?"

"Approximately ten thousand dollars."

"Over what period of time?"

"Over the last seventeen years."

He then said, "And that worked out to be how much per day?"

I told him that I wasn't sure and he asked, "What was this money to be used for?"

"I signed receipts saying that it was for reimbursement for food, cigarettes, taxis, and other expenses."

"Would it be safe to say that it was less than two dollars a day?"

To which I answered, "I think it was."

Tom was trying to present the jury with all of the facts that might possibly be misconstrued about me. He then played excerpts of videos and audio tapes that were recorded in my apartment.

As the prosecuting attorney questioned me, I made a point of looking at the jury as I answered them. Some of the jurors, to me, appeared to be in their twenties on up to others that looked like they were in their fifties. They seemed to be from all walks of life, both genders and several ethnicities. A truly wide range of people composed the group.

After finishing the excerpts, he asked me if what was presented in the tapes was a true and accurate account of the money I had paid to the defendants.

I answered, "Yes."

He asked me why I had paid them the money.

I told him that it was protection money. At that point, there were several objections from the defense attorneys. The judge told all of the attorneys to approach the bench for a sidebar. After a recess in questioning, Tom resumed his questions.

He asked me if I knew Steve Toushin. Ackerman objected. The judge sustained the objection, and Tom continued to ask me how much money I had given the defendant, Frank Schweihs.

After looking at the cheat sheet he had given me, I answered accurately. Then he asked me how much I had given to defendant Daddino. Again, I looked at my cheat sheet and answered accurately.

He asked me if I knew of a man named Louie Eboli, and I said, "Yes." He approached me with a picture of him and asked if that was him, and I said, "Yes."

He asked if I knew the relationship between Daddino and Eboli. John Sullivan immediately objected, and the objection was sustained.

There were numerous objections by John Sullivan, but we did get it on the record that I had seen and met with Louie Eboli and Daddino at the same time. I further stated that I knew about Eboli's death through the newspapers, which had labeled him an organized crime figure.

He asked me if I had any medical conditions. I told him I did, had panic attacks, and also suffered from agoraphobia. He asked me if I was taking any medication for it, right now while I was on the stand.

"Yes I am."

He asked me, "What would happen if you didn't take this medication?"

"I'm really not sure." at which point he asked me to describe what a normal panic attack was like.

I looked at the jury as I told the court,

"One time I had an attack while in my car, on my way to a business meeting, and I lost control and became disoriented and urinated all over myself. Then I returned home and failed to make the meeting. I stayed in my home for about a year, never leaving."

It wasn't long after these questions that Tom told the court that there were no more questions for this witness at this time. Numerous objections had been made during my testimony, and Judge Williams had sustained the objections, telling the jury that they were only to interpret my answers as "the witness's state of mind" as I answered.

Because of the numerous objections, Judge Williams had all attorneys meet at the bench for another sidebar. After about half an hour of discussions, she instructed the jury that they were excused for the day.

She then instructed me not to discuss the case with anyone: prosecutors or possible witnesses pertaining to this case.

After giving me those instructions, she recessed the court until the next day. She left the courtroom. I stood up and walked over to Tom Knight.

As we walked down the hallway, I asked Tom what was going on that made for such a long conversation with the judge and other lawyers. He told me that he couldn't discuss the case with me and that I couldn't talk about anything either.

Shortly thereafter, while Lenny and I were being transported from the court building by S/A Scott Jennings, in his car, Scott said to me, "What's the matter with you? You were supposed to tell him you were scared, scared for your life. The next time you step on the stand, that's what you are going to say!" Scott was angry as he told me these things.

I said to Scott, "Didn't the judge just tell us not to discuss these things?"

"I don't give a damn what the judge said. If this guy is acquitted, he'll kill you."

Lenny just sat there silently listening.

We returned the next day, and I again took the witness stand. The judge reminded me that I was still under oath. Tom asked me if I was afraid of the defendant, Frank Schweihs.

"No, because he's in custody."

He then asked me if I was ever afraid of him. I answered, "Yes," and he asked what I was afraid of.

"His reputation. His reputation as a hitman for the Outfit."

He clarified, "You mean organized crime?"

"Yes."

Alan Ackerman objected on the grounds of "hearsay" which was sustained. Tom then played another videotape excerpt that had taken place in my apartment, asking me, "Out of Frank's mouth, what did he tell you about his reputation?"

I replied, "He told me that his reputation preceded him."

He next asked what I perceived that reputation to be.

"He had a reputation of being a murderer."

Alan objected, and the judge turned to the jury and said, "This goes to the witness's state of mind."

Tom then proceeded to ask me questions about Daddino. They were almost identical to the ones he had asked me about Schweihs. When he asked me if I was ever afraid of Daddino, I said, "No."

He returned to questioning me about Schweihs, asking me if I was afraid of him. I answered, "I was afraid then, and I'm afraid now."

At that point, he said that he had no more questions for me. Court was adjourned for the day.

The next day the cross-examination took place in what long-time Chicago news reporter John Drummond described as my "baptism by fire," which is detailed in his book *Thirty Years in the Trenches*.

Alan Ackerman, who represented Frank, and John Sullivan, who represented Jeeps, asked me questions that they never should have asked.

Ackerman approached me, introducing himself. He then asked me if I had owned a business known as Chicago's Old Town Video.

I said, "Yes."

"What kind of business is this?"

"A licensed, adult-entertainment business, licensed by the city of Chicago."

He elaborated by asking me, "This is not the kind of business where you find members of the court or any members of the jury. Aren't you a smut peddler?"

"I'm not sure. Some of these people may be my customers. I don't know."

The courtroom cracked up, and some of the jury members smiled at my answer. My response had angered Alan. It also angered him that I would not look at him, since I was looking at the jurors in the jury box. On several occasions, he asked the judge to direct me to look at him instead of the jury. Judge Williams overlooked his requests and told him to continue with his examination.

John Sullivan gave a better cross examination but could not conceal the fact that Jeeps collected extortion money from me which was a clear violation of the Hobbs Act.

After each recess, when everyone stood up in the courtroom, and each of the jurors walked past me, several of them would nod at me. It seemed to me that they tried to say [without words], "We understand."

I think they were more impressed with the videotapes which I had made than about anything else that had been presented. The video and audio tapes were very graphic and provided them with a great insight into Frank's character and behavior.

Defense attorneys had received copies of copies of tapes during discovery, which were very grainy and difficult to see. But the originals were played in court and were crystal clear. The audio had left little room for misinterpretation regarding what Schweihs had said in our several exchanges. This, in my opinion, was a bit of a dirty trick by the prosecutors, but it was their call.

One thing I noticed during my testimony, an item that really stands out in my mind, was the fact that Frank's son, James, came in on the first day in a rather dapper suit and tie.

After the first day, his suit jacket was off, his tie was loosened, and he was no longer sitting up straight. One knee was now resting on the seat next to him. I remember thinking that this was the first time that he saw the "real" Frank Schweihs, his father. He seemed to be unravelling by the moment.

On the other hand, Frank's daughter, Nora, looked at me with her piercing eyes with no expression at all—emotionless and void of any trace of sympathy. Her empty, calculating composure and attitude were somehow more menacing and darker than if she had reacted in tears of sorrow as her father's exploits were shared in the courtroom. It sounds strange to describe, but it seemed as though she thought that I was the one who should be on trial instead of her father.

The contrasting reactions of these siblings really stood out to me and others who witnessed them during the court proceedings. Several comments were made about them and their differing behaviors.

Lenny took the stand right after me. The prosecution only asked him a few questions, one of which was, "Were you ever afraid of the defendants?"

"Yes, they were murderers!"

During the objections from both defense attorneys, Judge Williams turned to Lenny and said, "You're excused, unless the defense has any questions."

Both attorneys agreed that they had no questions for him. When she excused him, Judge Williams advised the jury that his statements should go to the witness's state of mind. I think the damage was already done, as to whether or not the defendants were innocent.

After several other witnesses had testified, the defense rested. With no surprise to me at all, the jury came back and convicted both men.

Judge Williams was more lenient with Daddino's sentencing of forty-five months and five years of probation; partly, I believe, because I had told her that I had never been afraid of Daddino, only the murderers he had associated with, when she asked it of me in the courtroom. He later appealed the sentence, and it was reduced to thirty-five months.

Frank, on the other hand, was sentenced to one hundred fifty-seven months [about thirteen years] for conspiracy and extortion. That was the maximum sentencing he could be given so she really threw the book at him. He also got his sentenced reduced, but it still remained a hefty one hundred twenty months.

After hearing the news, I walked down, unescorted, from the Dirksen Federal Building. Octoberfest was taking place in Chicago so I made my way through the crowd. Tom Knight followed me. We each grabbed a bratwurst and a beer. We congratulated each other on the trial and its outcome. I should also mention here that, other than my expenses of a total of $1.52 per day for the eighteen years I was undercover, I never received compensation for that trial. I returned home, thinking of what I was going to do with myself now that the trial had finally concluded. At this point, it was obvious that the alleged "million-dollar contract" on my life would never be fulfilled by Frank Schweihs.

I found out sometime later that television stations sued for the excerpts of the video tapes which were shown in court, under the Freedom of Information Act. They wanted to broadcast them in various news segments that would focus on the details of my many conversations in my apartment. They were never given copies, and their requests were denied.

Heck, I couldn't even get copies of them. I guess there are just some things the government doesn't feel it can trust us with, even though we have a legal right to them. Sometimes it makes you wonder who is really being protected—and who is being exploited. At least I took Frank off of the streets for a while, and he had been held without bond so he couldn't damage the case. Those were significant accomplishments for me, the agents, and attorneys who made it happen—and a major setback for Frank.

A Humorous Story
about Frank

Mark Rider was a young Chicago Police officer who was introduced to me by a sergeant who served with him. Mark was an unusual character with a very easy going personality. Mark always wore his ballistic vest and carried a .44 Magnum Smith & Wesson revolver in his shoulder holster. On the other side, underneath his arm, he carried another long-barreled revolver, his service revolver, and two back-up revolvers. On top of the pieces themselves, he carried more than enough ammunition to reload each of them. When I asked Mark why he carried so many guns, he said that he was in a shootout one time and was wounded because he had run out of ammunition. Needless to say, that wasn't going to happen to him again.

Whenever he showed up at a watch party in Lincoln Park, police officers, and people like myself, used to make jokes to him about how if he ever fell into the Lincoln Park Lagoon, he would drown because there was no way he could swim to the shore with the amount of weight that was on him. People I knew called him "Old Ironsides" and other names that referred to his armament. He was about six foot one, a trim 180 pounds, and took his job very seriously. He wasn't on the take. I am quite sure that if someone tried to bribe him, he would have arrested them. I really liked Mark because he was such a straight arrow.

Mark once told me that he had chased Frank Schweihs on a traffic violation. After several blocks of pursuit, Frank got a good distance between himself and Mark and abruptly pulled over into a legal parking stall. It was then that he got out of the car, locked it, and walked over to the parking meter attached to the spot and deposited a quarter. When Mark pulled up, he got out of the car and approached Frank, asking him to produce some identification. They argued, with Frank being his usual disrespectful self [without regard for the law], so Mark decided to call for backup.

When a supervisor arrived on the scene, he told Mark that he didn't have any probable cause to search the vehicle since it was parked legally and Frank was not in the car. Frank asked him if he had a warrant to search his vehicle and advised him what he could do with himself if he didn't have one.

I chuckled as Mark told me this story. Mark was naive. He didn't know that Frank was protected by his own commanding officers. Mark was made to feel bad that the incident even took place, by his superiors. They told him to back off and leave Frank alone. I told Mark that I knew Frank quite well, and he was a very dangerous man with high connections, not only with the Outfit but with the Chicago Police. He responded by shaking his head and saying, "It figures."

Another amusing incident involving Frank occurred on a Friday night outside of Frank's home, several doors down from my place. I had just chased a transvestite and "her" pimp away from the front of my property. They started doing business in Frank's driveway, stopping cars and soliciting their services to anyone who came by or would look at them.

Late that night, Frank came home with a driver. When Frank tried to enter his driveway, he was blocked by these two strange characters and a couple of their companions who immediately fled the scene. Frank and his driver got out of the car. It wasn't long before physical threats were exchanged between them and turned into actual violence.

I was in shock when I looked over there and saw Frank getting pummeled by a drag queen. Frank's driver hit the electric garage door opener and emerged moments later with a baseball bat. He took a swing at the pimp, missed, and was soon disarmed by his angry adversary. He then took a real beating by his own bat. I was laughing hysterically as I watched this all unfold—along with everyone else that witnessed it.

Seconds later, a Chicago Police squad car arrived on the scene. Two officers came out of the car, and everyone cooled off as they listened to the officers. They asked whose baseball bat it was. Frank insisted that it was his and that he had the right to defend himself. Another heated argument resulted, but this time it was with the police.

They arrested Frank for aggravated battery and took him away in the squad car. The rest of the people, who were standing around, were told to disperse, while the officers took Frank down to the 18th District Police Station for booking. There were no other arrests made at the scene.

Later on, and in keeping with his modus operandi, Frank appeared in court and had the charges dropped through a corrupt judge, JJ O'Donnell, and his representing attorney, Alan Ackerman. When I spoke to Frank about the incident, he gave me an entirely different story than the events I had personally witnessed. He told me that he was arrested on a UUW, the Unlawful Use of a Weapon [his baseball bat] charge. He said he got the best of the he/she and the charges were dropped in court.

I had a hard time keeping a straight face as he told me his version of the story, since I knew first hand that it was nothing like what I had seen. This feared Outfit hitman had been beaten up by an effeminate street urchin. How ironic for such a tough guy. He must have had too much to drink that night.

As usual, the record was expunged. I don't even know if there is a police report in existence today about it, but I do know that police officers talked about it a lot. We all got a good laugh at Frank's expense. Only in Chicago.

THE DEATH OF BEVERLY HANSEN

Shortly after testifying in federal court on the Schweihs' case, I was in contact with Danny Hansen. He was one of the few people who had my SkyPager number if he needed to connect.

I was stunned when Danny told me that his mother, Beverly Rae Hansen, was dead. He began to tell me that he thought there was something odd in the way she died because his other family members withheld the fact that the cause of her death was hanging and ruled a suicide. Even more shocking was the fact that Danny's birthday was just days away. Knowing Bev as I did, I knew she was not the type of woman who would stage such a bitterly ironic event for her firstborn son.

I told Danny that I would look into it and get to the bottom of it. Danny was extremely concerned about the fact that she left no will or suicide note.

Over the phone Danny told me how upset he was with his father and brother. He had no prior knowledge of his mother's death until close friends of the family came to pick him up the afternoon of the wake, at which time he was told that she had died of a heart attack. He saw his mother lying in the coffin wearing a dress that she absolutely hated. It was a green Tudor-necked dress that completely concealed noose-marks on her neck.

Close friends and a family member told him the reason for the dress was so other people would not see those marks. He was then told that his mother had committed suicide by hanging herself.

Danny said, "I ain't buyin' this shit! There's no way mom would have killed herself, much less hanged herself!"

I also learned that she had been cremated immediately after the wake. I told him that I'd get copies of the police reports and find the truth about what had really happened.

I then contacted a detective at the Country Club Hills Police Department who told me that he could not give out any information over the phone—and that I should come into his office. I told him this was impossible; not only was I not in the area but due to the fact that I had recently testified against a major Mob figure from Chicago, I knew that my return could cost me my life.

I contacted my buddy, "Jimmy D" James DeLorto of the Bureau of Alcohol, Tobacco, Tax, and Firearms, and asked him if he would get copies of the police reports and forward them to me.

I first met James Delorto right after he had arrested Mikey Swiatek and John Bamboolis for possession of an altered firearm [a sawed off shotgun and a machine gun—MAC 11 with a silencer on it] and 2 kilos of cocaine. Jimmy D was the ATF's Supervisor for Chicago and had requested a meeting with me through the U.S. Attorney's office. They called the FBI and had my handler at the time, Hank Schmidt, let me know that he wanted to meet with me. He didn't know who I was as he simply knew I was "Red from Wells Street."

Hank strongly advised me against meeting with Jimmy, but I told him that I wanted to, despite his protests. He told me that he couldn't stop me from going and I said, "That's good 'cause I'm goin' anyway!"

Tom Knight, the Chicago Strike Force Assistant U.S. Attorney, and I were in the room of the Holiday Inn on Madison and Halstead in the early afternoon when Jimmy knocked on our door. Tom and I were dressed in suits. Jimmy was in plain clothes, just like a mob guy. Tom introduced Jimmy to me, and as we shook hands, he asked me if the "Feebs" [FBI] were paying for room. When I told they were, he said, "As long as it's on them, then let's eat!" He then asked me to pick up the phone and order a pot of coffee. I ordered some Danishes to accompany the coffee along with some milk for myself.

We talked about a lot of things, but he told me that the main reason he wanted to meet with me was to find out what I knew about the Grand Avenue Crew—and if I knew Mike Swiatek.

"Yea, sure I know Mikey. He's part of our crew and a demolition expert."

Jimmy said, "How do you know he's a demolition expert?"

I told him about several of the buildings which he had demolished and particularly about the job he'd done next to Jimmy Cozzo's place. Jimmy had told me that when the explosion happened, the reclining chair he was asleep in went about three feet into the air and scared him half to death until he realized what was going on.

Jimmy D and I talked for hours about the Grand Avenue Crew. He told he recognized me from "undercover buys" in the past, as I had made hand-grenade and machine-gun parts purchases on behalf of the ATF. We had a lot in common and hit it off right from the start. I implicitly trusted him. He was so covert and silent that I knew I could tell him anything, and it would stay with him, in confidence.

We laughed, told jokes, and talked for four or five hours. He viewed his time with me as time well spent, as I gave him information he couldn't get elsewhere. Tom Knight was scratching his head a lot and couldn't believe all of the things we discussed, especially the historical timelines and events we had common knowledge of.

When the meeting concluded, Jimmy gave me his business card and told me, "Let's keep in touch, buddy." I told him we'd do that, and he left.

Tom told me he'd give me a call on Monday. Tom and I waited a while before leaving so that we didn't cause a scene.

One thing Jimmy D asked me that really stood out to me during our day's conversation was, "How much of a reward are you getting from the FBI for your information?"

I told him they weren't paying me anything at all.

"You really got screwed! Those cheap bastards! You'd a made a fortune if you'd a gone with us rather than working with the Feebs. We'd a taken care a ya!"

At the time, I really didn't think too much of it as business was booming. Money was not an issue, but it did feel gratifying to know that another government agency thought well of me and appreciated my work.

When I read the official police report Jimmy D had procured for me, the sworn statements of Mark Hansen, Danny's younger brother, truly disturbed me. His sworn statement was totally inconsistent with his normal vernacular. Something seemed suspicious about it, which later proved to be true.

After reading the reports over and over and having had numerous telephone conversations, Jimmy DeLorto asked me a lot of questions about the "Chicago Horse Mafia." He was surprised to hear that I knew most of the players. When he mentioned the name of Bob Brown, he asked me how I knew him. I told him that I met Bob, and Kathy his wife, through Kenneth Hansen. As a matter of fact, I told him that through Ken Hansen I had met all of the people who he had asked me about.

Jimmy was impressed with some of my background knowledge about those under investigation in connection with Helen Brach's disappearance. Jimmy knew that my main focus for eighteen years, as a mole for the FBI, was organized crime and that I had a very exhaustive knowledge of the Chicago Mob.

As we spoke further, he brought up Ken Hansen's name again, curious about any crimes that he may have committed. I told him that he had burned down Forest View Stable several times and his brother Curt was a hit man for the Chicago Outfit.

He was also trying to pick my brain to see if we could get anybody on the list to flip and turn state's evidence on the Helen Brach murder. Ken's name was on the list to appear before the grand jury. He was ducking its subpoena but had no idea that he was about to be arrested for the Schuessler-Peterson murders.

At that point, I told Jimmy, "He claims to have killed three boys in 1955 on the north side of Chicago, when he was 22 years old."

This peaked Jimmy's interest.

"How do you know?"

"I don't know for sure. I wasn't there, that's what Hansen told me. But it doesn't make any difference anyway because that's just hearsay."

"Did he tell you he did it or did you hear that from someone else?"

"No, he told me about it on numerous occasions."

"What did he tell you? Did he tell you he did it or did you hear that from someone else? What did he tell you?" he said as he latched onto my statements like an unrelenting leach.

I told him that the most outstanding thing that I remembered was that he referred to it as "The Peterson Boys" and the fact that he had strangled them.

Jimmy asked me how old I was in 1955. I told him that I was about 6 years old. He asked me if I'd ever been to any libraries or had looked up any newspaper clippings about the case.

"Why would I? It's only hearsay anyway." I again affirmed.

Jimmy insisted that it was not hearsay when someone tells you what they have done.

"That's a confession, Red!"

I retorted, "That's not what the FBI told me!"

After a long and heated debate, I learned that Hansen had made numerous confessions to me about a lot of different things. Jimmy asked me if I would work with an ATF agent on this case which he referred to as the "The Schuessler/Peterson Murders."

That was the first time I had heard the name of Schuessler in connection with this case. I asked if I'd be working with him, and he said, "No, I have to find the right guy for the job."

Seated at Left John Rotunno, Jimmy Grady at back with Sultan,
Jimmy Delorto at Right

Sometime later, Jimmy introduced me to John N. Rotunno of the ATF, the finest federal agent who I have ever worked with on any case. John asked me more questions than anyone had in my entire life. He kept copies of notes during all of our interviews which took place face to face.

This was the inception of how a forty-year-old triple homicide was solved, tried, and convicted. This cold case file had begun to thaw.

Jimmy DeLorto and John Rotunno spoke to me numerous times over the telephone, comparing facts that I had given them. Sometime later John and Jimmy interviewed me again. At that time, I was told that every fact that I had previously given them had been researched and verified as correct.

One of the questions that was asked of me in an earlier interview was if I had ever discussed this with anyone or knew of anyone else that had knowledge of the murders.

"The only person that I know of is Roger Spry, who had lived with Ken Hansen for a long period of time."

Upon my next face-to-face interview, I met with John Rotunno of the ATF; Jimmy Grady of the ATF; Patrick J. Quinn, an Assistant State's Attorney of the Cook County Organized Crime Division; Scott Cassidy, also an Assistant State's Attorney of the Cook County's Organized Crime Division; and Lou Rabbit, a Chicago Police Officer. The six of us met in a small hotel room. To say that it was crowded is an understatement.

Scott Cassidy was leaning against the wall in the corner of the room, and Pat Quinn was sprawled out all over the bed. As for me, I was just looking for a place to sit. Pat Quinn did most of the talking, asking me questions that I had already answered for the ATF agents.

THE PITIABLE ACCOUNT OF
ROGER SPRY

At a later time, I was told by John Rotunno that an arrest warrant had been issued for Roger Spry for the arson of Forest View Stables, which was one of the many facts that I had given them. Some months later, in July of 1994, Roger Spry was arrested in Arizona on an unrelated charge. After fingerprinting him and doing a name check on NCIC, the local law enforcement department in Maricopa County, Arizona, saw that he had an outstanding warrant in Chicago.

Upon learning this fact, John Rotunno, Lou Rabbit, Scott Cassidy, and Pat Quinn flew out to interview Roger. From what I understand, Roger had a bit too much to drink when they arrived to question him, so they stayed overnight and spoke to him the next day. It was at that time that Roger admitted that he had committed the arson at Forest View Stables.

Roger had no intentions of spending time in prison. The county jail was one thing, but prison was another. Roger volunteered valuable information at this time to everyone who was there. He basically corroborated everything that I had told the ATF about the Schuessler/Peterson murders.

In specific detail, he described how he met Ken Hansen, at ten years of age, and how he was sleeping in the hay loft of his barn because he had no parental supervision. His father was away in West Virginia, and his mother was a local prostitute. He had run away from his unhappy home and eventually found Ken. Roger then told of how he moved in with Ken and Bev at 79th and Harlem, in their apartment, along with the Hansen's sons, Danny and Mark, who were approximately four and two years of age at that time.

Shortly thereafter, the Hansen family moved to the Broken H Stables at 82nd and Keene Avenue. When Roger spurned Ken's sexual advances, he was forced to sleep downstairs in the dog kennels. Beverly was a registered AKC breeder of a fine line of Dobermans and used the kennels for her business. In the room was a small single bed. He said that the smell was so bad that it could gag a maggot. Roger kept a window open for fresh air but that didn't help very much. All this time, Bev had no idea what terrible atrocities her husband was perpetrating on Roger and the other young boys in and around the stables.

Through a series of circumstances, Roger told Ken Hansen's hidden secrets of his pedophilic, homosexual practices to numerous people in the neighborhood. As a result of the rumors, a close personal friend of Ken's, by the name of Mike Burns, rushed over to the Broken H one night and started screaming to Ken about how Roger was runnin' off his mouth to everyone in the area.

Roger stayed hidden in his dog kennel dungeon, in fear of his life, and barricaded the door with cases of pop bottles that were stored in the room. Kenny told Mike to go and get Roger so Mike crashed through the door, smashing the bottles, and scattering shards of glass everywhere. He grabbed Roger by the throat and began to choke him. With all of the debris and lack of good lighting, Roger escaped from his clutches and ran into the woods behind the stables. He stayed hidden until Mike had left.

Several hours later Roger returned to his meager abode to clear a little of the glass from his bed and began to try and sleep. Ken Hansen came into his room and sat on his bed, speaking words of comfort, telling Roger that Mike wasn't going to hurt him.

Before he knew it, his pants were pulled down, and Kenny was committing fellatio on him. The next day something amazing happened; he was now living in a bedroom of the home instead of the kennels. This appeared to be the beginning of a dedicated homosexual relationship between the two of them, which Ken cultivated by his twisted, exploitive system of rewards.

For the next seven years, Roger not only bedded with Ken Hansen but committed numerous crimes for him, as a minor. This assured Ken that he could never be arrested for the things that he sent Roger to do—and kept Roger in fear of legal authorities. Arsons, thefts, vandalisms, beatings, and sundry other crimes were committed by him at the bequest of Hansen.

Roger was never prosecuted because the Chief of Detectives of Markham City always interfered in the arrests, abusing his authority as a favor to Ken, in exchange for assistance with other questionable ventures such as the murder of George Jayne, half-brother of the notorious Silas Jayne.

The attention and love-starved Roger, just like an orphaned street urchin from Charles Dicken's *Oliver Twist*, became a modern day victim of a predatory Fegan whose main purpose was to exploit young boys for his own deviant pleasures and criminal activities.

As a teen, Roger was told by Kenny that he had picked up three young kids hitchhiking on the North side of Chicago, and took them to a stable owned by Silas Jayne. He went on to tell Roger that it had always been his thing to have sex with two boys at the same time, that this was his fantasy.

As fate would have it, it didn't work out for Kenny. After sexually molesting one of the boys, Ken Hansen's worst fear occurred as the three boys started to leave, telling Hansen that they were going to tell their parents and the police. Kenny grabbed the oldest boy in a chokehold with his right arm around his neck, leaving his left arm free to keep the younger boys from getting away. While the boys were screaming and scrambling to get away, he choked the oldest kid to death.

Hansen said he had no other choice but to kill the other two kids. Kenneth Hansen had purged his conscience to Roger Spry of how he murdered the Schuessler and Peterson boys, all while downing a bottle of Chivas Regal Scotch. His story and testimony so closely paralleled my own encounter with Ken that the authorities had a good idea of the modus operandi employed by Ken.

Pat Quinn and his entourage, armed with Roger's statement, caught a jet back to Chicago. They secured a warrant for Ken Hansen's arrest for the arson of Forest View Stables, as there was no statute of limitations for arson, kidnapping, or murder. Kenny was finally going to have to pay for some of the terrible things he had done.

KENNETH HANSEN IS FINALLY BROUGHT TO JUSTICE

On the 11th of August, 1994, law enforcement officers from the ATF, Chicago Police Department, and Country Club Hills surrounded Ken Hansen's home at 18761 South Cicero Ave. in Country Club Hills in order to arrest him. During their surveillance of Hansen's home, Kenny called Jimmy Tynan, one of his pedophilic cohorts who lived next door. The phone call was monitored on the other extension in Jimmy's own home, by a law enforcement [ATF] agent.

Jimmy Tynan was instructed by federal authorities not to tell Kenneth Hansen that anything was wrong, that it was safe to come home. Sometime after the call, towards 1:00 a.m. the following morning, Kenny drove up in his son Mark's pickup truck, loaded with two large suitcases in the back. It was obvious to the police that he was getting ready to leave town. I later learned he was going to make a run for Shawnee National Forest where Mark Hansen had purchased some land through his own financial benefits that were associated with his mother's death.

When Ken Hansen walked into his home, he took a seat on his couch and asked Jimmy Tynan to get him a cup of hot tea, which he did. When Ken, relieved to finally be safe at home, began sipping his tea, several ATF agents, Chicago Police Officers, Cook County Police Officers, Country Club Hills Police Officers, and State's Attorney's Police Officers sprang from their hiding places with pistols drawn while yelling at him to put his hands up and not to move.

I was told that Kenny was so scared that he jumped up suddenly from the sofa, spilling the hot tea on his lap, and immediately complied with their orders. He had a look of genuine terror on his face as the authorities confronted him. To say the least, he was not expecting the encounter and was caught off guard.

He was likely thinking, "All this for a subpoena?" Little did he know the true reason for their efforts, but he would soon find out. This arrest was all a well-coordinated effort by all involved departments, in company of two Assistant State's Attorneys. Kenny was transported into the custody of authorities for interrogation.

In the beginning of Hansen's interview, he was asked if he knew Roger Spry, Bobby Stitt, Joe Plemmons, and me.

"Yes, I know them. They're all fine young men, friends of mine." Hansen affirmed.

Then the officer asked him if he knew that they were going to testify against him. Suddenly his demeanor changed.

"They are all liars and would say anything to hurt me. I spurned their affections towards me!"

Kenny confirmed that he was gay and was also a pedophile. He admitted that, over the years, he had molested more than one thousand boys, a fact that was not admissible in court owing to the fact that it had no relevance to his current charges. Kenny soon began to see that his interview was not going where he had anticipated. He began to ask for his lawyer. He was told that his lawyer was not the one that would be doing time. The police then got much more physical with him, in an effort to extract more information and confessions from him.

They continued to interview Hansen and announced his capture to the various media outlets, at which time every news station in Chicago had a lead story of his arrest for the then thirty-nine-year-old, unsolved homicides of the three boys. The older audiences who remembered the horrific crime were surely shocked to hear that the perpetrator was now in custody.

* * *

Kenneth Hansen had been charged in the coldest case in the history of the United States. It later spawned other offices to begin opening their own cold-case units. This was one case that police officers never thought would be solved.

Anton Schuessler, eleven years of age, John Schuessler, thirteen, and Robert Peterson, aged fourteen, were the boys named in the record. Their brutal murders had literally changed the average, post-1955 American family's perceptions of the world. According to local news stations in 1955, over 3,270 potential suspects were interviewed in connection with this case. Two hundred forty-four of those suspects were also given lie detector tests. Finally, after almost forty years, an arrest was made for the murders of these three boys.

Justice would, at least eventually, be served.

HERB HOLLATZ GETS INVOLVED

Ten news media went rampant with lead stories about the Peterson, Schuessler Murders. One station, WGN, which broadcast on cable TV throughout the country, carried it as a lead story for several days. This caught the eyes of several other people who had knowledge of the crime and had since moved away from the Chicagoland area.

Herb Hollatz was born on September 16th, 1931. He had been a friend of Ken Hansen's since the latter half of 1952. His father was a Chicago Police Detective. In January of 1956, Herb moved out west and had settled there, where he married and had six children.

Kenneth Hansen, Arrest Area 6 1994

In 1994, Herb learned of Hansen's case while in his Arizona home watching WGN cable news. He was startled when he saw that Kenneth Hansen had been arrested for the murders of the Peterson, Schuessler boys. At that time, he must have reflected back upon all of the events of 1955, the news media coverage, and the intensive police investigation to capture the murderer. After all, he was one of the many Chicago-area residents who had been interviewed by the police. He subsequently called his daughter to tell her that he had already known about the murders that Hansen had committed.

He was not half as startled to see the news reported as he was when, on Saturday, April 8, 1995, Pat Quinn, Jimmy Grady, and John Rotunno arrived at his home. Herb had known Beverly Hansen quite well when he was in his early twenties. He also knew Kenny quite well; well enough to allow Kenny to perform oral sex on him.

After such an intimate moment, Ken asked him to do him a favor and to promise not to say anything to anyone about what he was going to tell him. Herb promised. Hansen then confessed to Herb that he had just killed three boys. Herb Hollatz knew that the three boys that he was talking about were the Schuessler brothers and Bobby Peterson.

Herb had asked Kenny, "Why did you do that?"

Ken Hansen replied that somebody had told him to do it. Ken also told him not to tell anybody—or his brother Curtis would kill him. Herb was only too aware of Curt Hansen's reputation as a mob hit man and enforcer. He certainly believed that if he would've told Ken Hansen's secret, then he would've been killed by Curt.

About two weeks after Kenny's confession to Herb, the police arrived at The Rancho Russell Stable where Herb boarded his horse. The police questioned him if he had any knowledge that could help their investigation of the murder of three boys. He said he didn't know anything about it.

Shortly after the encounter with the Chicago Police, Ken Hansen said that he knew that they were out near Herb's area, questioning people. He asked Herb if he'd said anything. Herb adamantly replied, "Definitely, I did not!"

Herb Hollatz was terrified and embarrassed that his father, the police detective, would find out that he had engaged in a homosexual encounter with Ken Hansen. He knew for sure that his father wouldn't have been very happy about it. The information he was hiding about the murders, most certainly contributed to his decision to relocate himself out west.

I was told that Herb's fear of Curt Hansen was so intense that before he was willing to testify against Kenny, ATF agents had to supply him with a copy of Curt's death certificate and a photo of his gravesite. Agents flew back to Chicago, took the picture of his tombstone at the VA cemetery, and made a copy of Curt's death certificate.

They presented both items as proof positive of Curt's death and left them to Herb for inspection. After resolving his concern, Herb Holitz became a fully cooperating witness. He provided a written statement to a court stenographer, under sworn oath. Armed with this new information, this was yet another nail in the coffin for the trial. It also bears mentioning here that, upon completion of the case, newscasts featured jurors who said that Herb Hollatz was the most convincing witness of the entire trial.

I Arrive for the Trial

After a few motions by the defense attorneys, Judge Toomin made his decision on what would be allowed in court, and it was off to Chicago for me. The ATF was so worried about my security that they came to my home and personally drove me back to Chicago.

As we drove along the Interstate, armed men with fully automatic weapons were on some overpasses. There was a car in front of us while another trailed behind us. The vehicle that followed us featured an armed guard carrying an MP5. Each state supplied a support team of ATF agents along the route, and it was all masterfully coordinated. They stayed with me in the motels on our stops. I wasn't allowed to leave my motel room at any time. They brought food to my room for me to consume with my daily medication and agents accompanied me through the entire excursion as we made it back to my native turf.

The reason for their overprotective nature was the fact that I had been the key witness in the Frank Schweihs' trial. Everyone was worried about an attempt on my life as a measure of retaliation from the Outfit. There was a murder contract on my life at that time for a full million dollars. Needless to say, that kind of money is very tempting—even for "friends."

We arrived at a safe location near Chicago, and I was exhausted as we walked up the steps into the building. Somebody offered me some coffee, but I was looking for some water to drink. I was then introduced to the Special Agent in Charge [SAC] of the facility where we were staying.

He immediately began giving me a run-down of all of the things I could and couldn't do which gave me a real impression that I was basically being put under house arrest. The things I could do were so miniscule and the things I couldn't do were so ticky-tack that they even included reading the Chicagoland Yellow Pages. My mood was not exactly pleasant after that long ride to get there, so my language was not very polite. I basically told him he was full of bullshit if he thought I would go along with all of his rules for me.

I left the building unescorted and began walking down the street, looking for a pay phone to use to call a couple of friends who lived nearby that had offered to help me out if I needed to leave the care of federal authorities. Moments later, several agents caught up to me, and one grabbed me by the shoulder to turn me around. I jerked my arm away, releasing his grip in the process, and told him to keep his hands off of me.

Someone stopped and talked to him. They started a dialogue with me to convince me to calm down and be a bit more sympathetic to the agents who were there to ensure my safety. I decided to give them another chance.

As we returned into the building, we went into the SAC's office. The other agents explained, to him, that I was not a prisoner and was there of my own choosing rather than from the compulsive influence of the law. The SAC's demeanor and approach to running the place reminded me of Marine Corp boot-camp. My single fond memory of my time there: graduation day.

I learned he was also a former Marine. He finally toned down his approach with me and began treating me like a normal human being rather than a convict or criminal. We eventually became good friends as we discussed different cases we had each been involved with and shared our life experiences with each other. A bit of respect and understanding can really go a long way if you want to get along with someone.

HOTEL SECURITY DETAILS

John Rotunno, Jimmy Grady, and another agent named Dave [LNU] had accompanied me through the trip. We all got the rules of how we would approach and deal with one another straightened out before relocating to a Chicagoland Marriott hotel. Two agents went into the hotel and cleared the lobby of customers before I made my entry into the elevator. The elevator had its own camera which provided a comprehensive view of the hallway leading to my room.

The Feds had rented the entire top floor, and there were agents all along the hallways as I passed by their command post, the room just next to mine. All of their heavy handed security measures seemed like overkill for a single witness. I would later find out that ALL of the witnesses were staying in that same hotel.

They asked me if I wanted anything to eat, and I told them, "Yeah, I want some Italian beef sandwiches!" I was really looking forward to some since I couldn't get any in my new hometown.

When they asked me how many I wanted, I said, "Give me eight of them, complete with sweet peppers and fries!" Their eyes opened wide. They asked if I was sure of that, and I confirmed they had heard me correctly as they went out to get them. To the surprise of everyone but myself, I finished each one of them—all the way down to the last French fry.

I got rather thirsty after my enormous meal and realized that I hadn't ordered anything to drink so I went down the hallway to get some ice out of the ice machine to put into my water. I left without their taking notice of me. An agent must have seen me on one of the several surveillance cameras which the ATF had installed in the elevator, command post, and hallways. He caught up to me, informing me that they just couldn't let me wander around unescorted. I told them I just needed some ice. They told me that they would get me anything I needed, if I just asked them for it.

I told them that I needed the exercise and that I would get it myself. It was getting close to the time for the evening news, and when I turned on my TV, the upcoming case was all over the stations. I laid back in my bed while watching the news and fell asleep.

PREPARATIONS FOR THE TRIAL

It wasn't until the next weekend that I was taken to the Cook County Courthouse. I had never been there previously and wanted to see what things would be like when the trial began. I wanted to be familiar with everything prior to the court proceedings that I would be involved in as a witness. Scott Cassidy also wanted me to be familiar with everything, too.

When we arrived there, we went through a maze of security gates through a small side-door leading to an elevator. There were about nine of us who entered the elevator. The elevator operator, a Cook County Deputy and Officer of the Court, took us up to our floor.

As we got out of the elevator, I said, "I'm not coming in this building again that way, and I am certainly not walking up the front steps. The security around here stinks. Do you know who that guy is?"

They replied with a simple, "Who?"

I told them that the Deputy who was operating the elevator was connected to the Chicago Mob, and that in the past, I had given him payoffs for his services.

They told me not to worry because he would not be in the building again, at least not while I was there.

They showed me the courtroom. We visited the witness room and the corridors that I would have to walk down on the trial date. We discussed the case as we walked around the empty building and then went into Scott Cassidy's office to go over a few of the finer points.

I couldn't help but notice an enlarged photo, four feet by eight feet, of the dead boys which had been taken at the crime scene. It was mounted on an easel that was going to be brought into the courtroom as evidence.

I looked at it and saw the naked little boys laying on the ground, bodies entwined around one another in a heap. I was very upset at the image, and I had only looked at it through peripheral vision because it was such a horrific scene. I was so taken aback with it that I vomited into the sink in Scott's office.

In the car, on the way back to the hotel, I hesitantly asked Jimmy Grady what I thought was a very strange, even embarrassing, question.

"Jimmy, I didn't look at that photo very well because it made me sick but were any of those boys in that big photo sexually mature?"

Jimmy Grady, a former sex crime investigator and expert, told me, "No, in those days, children did not mature at that early of an age."

I just sat there in the car thinking that this was all much worse than I had ever thought it was. There is a big difference between talking about something versus confronting it in graphic detail. Looking back, I am sure that it also had a dramatic effect on the jury.

THE FIRST TRIAL OF
KENNETH HANSEN

The trial began, and I was able to watch its proceedings on the local news. Agents were careful to keep me on schedule with my medication and catered to my needs while we waited for my turn to testify. The morning I was to testify, they walked me out of the hotel and into a van for transport to the courthouse.

Six agents were in the van. I saw several MP5 machine guns that were locked and loaded, in case they were needed. Three other vehicles accompanied us to the Cook County Courthouse, and all of us were waved on at the security checkpoints. It seemed they knew I was coming and were ready for anything.

As we went deeper into the compound that surrounded the courthouse, leading to the same side door that I had previously used to enter the building, we noticed that all of the news cameramen with telescopic lenses were making every effort to get me on videotape. They got footage of the entourage, but that was it.

When the doors to the van opened, there were over a dozen agents dressed in blue jeans, suits, and other clothing so that they would look like they fit into the crowd. Four of the agents in my van exited wearing bullet-proof jackets and completely surrounded the exit of the van. The other two followed me out, and I was surrounded as they walked me to the door.

I was told later, by news reporters, that they couldn't get a clear shot of me, even with a telephoto lens. My escort had been so tightly aligned that it had made it nearly impossible to catch so much as a glimpse of me.

As our large group walked to the elevator, it was apparent that all of us would not be able to fit into it at the same time, even though it was a freight elevator. I operated the elevator and stopped it on the courtroom floor. When I opened the doors, there was no one in sight as we surveyed the corridors that led to the courtroom.

As we walked through the passageways, I was told that the courtroom doors were locked so that no one could come out from the courtroom. This surprised me. It wasn't long before I was in the witness room behind the judge's chambers, waiting to testify. I was watching the courtroom proceedings on the closed-circuit TV there and was guarded by two ATF agents. One of them was a gorgeous gal who really went the extra mile for me and was as pleasant as anyone could possibly be.

When my name was called, I entered the courtroom. The lady agent followed me into the courtroom. As I took my oath on the witness stand, she pulled up a chair and sat right next to me. As she did so, the male agent stood to the other side of her, with his back against the wall. It is important to note, at this time, that both agents' sidearms were visible to anyone in the courtroom.

As I sat down and looked into the crowd of spectators, it was speckled with agents. My direct testimony by Scott Cassidy went as expected and was now complete.

When the defense counsel, Jed Stone, questioned me on redirect, he asked me, "Who is that young lady sitting next to you? Have you discussed this case with her?"

I replied with a firm, "No."

Frustrated with my answer, he asked me many different questions, some pertaining to the trial of an organized crime figure who I had helped put away. There were several sidebars at which Judge Toomin ruled that my present identity was not to be revealed.

After I had completed my testimony, the judge adjourned court for the day. Most of the spectators left through the courtroom door, leaving approximately twelve agents remaining in the court. As I started back towards the witness room and the safe exit, they followed me.

Jed Stone was right beside us. He made some comments to the gal who had been sitting next to me through my testimony. One of the male agents, from the crowd, said, "Don't forget us, you prick! We were here all the time."

We all had to wait until they had transported Ken Hansen past us, to the jail elevator. I couldn't help but see the jailers banging his head off of the wall as he tripped and fell in his baggy business suit. At that moment, I couldn't help but feel sorry for him as I watched him being abused. I could see that he was injured. I knew he was guilty of a lot of terrible things, but that didn't make his suffering enjoyable to me.

I was whisked out of the building, as my testimony was now over, to a car which drove me back to the hotel. We packed up my suitcase, and the ATF agents started to drive me back home.

A few hours later, while we were out on the open road, one of them had a call on their cell phone. We all learned, from that call, that the jury only took forty-five minutes to come back with a guilty verdict on all three counts of murder. We were all laughing because we knew that the jury took thirty minutes for lunch. It sure didn't take much time for them to make up their minds!

At Ken Hansen's sentencing hearing, the judge sentenced him to three hundred years without parole. Under the sentencing guidelines from when the crime took place, in 1955, he would have been sentenced to death by an electric chair. Because he was arrested in the 1990s, the death penalty had been repealed. When the legislators wrote the law to repeal it, they put in a paragraph stating that under their new guidelines, the defendant could have his choice of either the current parameters or the guidelines in place when the crime was committed. Ken Hansen chose the guidelines at the time of his arrest under the hope that he could have a lighter sentence.

Just before he was sentenced, the judge asked him if he had anything to say. He approached the bench stating that, "I am the only victim here. I did not commit these crimes." It was obvious that his words fell on deaf ears.

John Rotunno, along with Jimmy Grady, had been gathering information from April 19, 1993 to August 11, 1994, in preparation for this arrest, trial, and subsequent conviction. Over sixteen months of good investigative work of the ATF was not done in vain. The prosecutors for the state were Scott Cassidy and Pat Quinn with Tom Biesty assisting from their office. They made a solid case, and the resulting conviction came as no surprise to anyone.

A Professor Tries to
Make a Point

I was filled with disgust and anger, for many reasons, when the
appellate court later overturned Ken Hansen's conviction because
the prosecution entered evidence of pedophilia and homosexual acts
which had taken place decades after the crime had taken place. They set a
retrial date in the year 2000. ATF agent John Rotunno told me this would
happen several years earlier—and he was right.

Art O'Donnell, Ken's family attorney, had passed away, and Leonard
Goodman, a DePaul University Law Professor, took Ken's case pro bono,
leaving all of his students to investigate a strategy to win the case. This was
a major mistake by Professor Goodman. I asked Scott Cassidy if this case
was going to be tougher because Goodman was a law professor, unlike
Hansen's previous legal representation.

He chuckled and said, "You have nothing to worry about. This guy is
going to be a piece of cake."

It wasn't long after that and Scott said to me, over the phone, that
they had the right to depose me [ask me questions], but I had the right to
remain silent if there was anything I didn't want to answer. Even so, I told
him that I would be glad to do it telephonically.

Scott arranged for them to be in his office when he called. There
were a number of Goodman's students present for the conversation. After
hearing questions from his students, which were not at all pertinent to the
case, I said, "I don't wanna talk to you anymore. Ya had your shot to talk
to me. I gave it to you, and you are all a bunch of idiots!"

With that Scott hung up the phone.

In the weeks to come Scott Cassidy told me that Leonard Goodman
filed a motion before Judge Mary Ellen Coughlan stating that Scott

Cassidy had never given him, personally, the opportunity to depose me. In his motion he also said that he wanted a court order for me to be in Chicago to be deposed.

Scott called me and told me the results of the hearing. I would have to come to Chicago. To say the least, this really upset me. I felt that I had been more than fair in making myself available to the defense, but the judge had ruled, so I had to comply.

I went back to Chicago and met with Scott in the State's Attorney's Office, at which time he told me that Leonard Goodman was going to see me the next day. To me, it was just going through the motions.

The next morning, I was disturbed that Scott would not be accompanying me to the deposition and sent me with a Deputy State's Attorney in his stead. Let me make it clear for anyone unfamiliar with this occupation: a Deputy State's Attorney is not a lawyer: he is a police officer with a badge and gun who gets assignments by the State's Attorney. We walked into a room with a long table and several chairs. I sat down at the head.

About half an hour later, a man walked into the room saying, "I'm Leonard Goodman." as he stretched out his hand to shake mine. "You must be Red!" he said with a smile on his face.

He was very friendly towards me. He asked me to excuse him because his stenographer was late and would be in momentarily. His investigator was named Ernie Rizzo and was known to have done a lot of work for the Outfit.

I told him, "You don't need a stenographer."

He told me that was okay and that we could just get started.

"Well let's start in the beginning. What day did you get out of the Marine Corps?"

I answered him by saying, "I don't want to talk about it."

He asked me several other questions, to which he got the same response. I was waiting for someone to object to his line of questions, but it wasn't going to happen, as there was no one there acting on my behalf.

I told him, "There aren't any questions that you can ask me that I want to answer."

He replied, "Would you like to speak to my investigator?" who was seated next to him.

I said, "I know Ernie, and I got nothin' to say to him—or you!"

At that moment, the room went silent.

Feeling awkward, I said, "In a few moments I am going to stand up and take my jacket and leave, but before I do, I have something to say."

I stood up and expressed my true feelings and stated, "This is not about the truth. This is about which lawyer is a better lawyer who can win his case. It disgusts me."

And with that I got up and left the room and returned to Scott's office.

Scott was very upset by the statement that I had made, fearing that it would be used against me in court. I was angry that he had not accompanied me for the exchange. I told him not to worry about it, and that if he asked me any questions about my statement, I was sure I could handle it. That afternoon, I left for my home, having complied with my court order.

The next time I returned to Chicago, it was for the second trial. This time I returned under my own steam and checked into a motel, with the aid of the ATF. For a few days I roamed the streets of Chicago in a rented car and called on various old friends who took me out with them as we enjoyed meals, movies, and each other's company. It sure beat sitting in a hotel room waiting for them to call me.

THE RETRIAL OF
KENNETH HANSEN

The business of this trial was a whole lot easier than Hansen's first case. Some of the witnesses from the first trial had passed away, and they had to read their previous testimonies from that trial into this one.

John Osborne, my first FBI handler, was subpoenaed to testify by Tom Biesty. He came to Chicago with an attorney whom the FBI provided him with. The FBI didn't want the retired agent to testify, so they objected to the State Court calling him to the stand. John had called me and told me he remembered what I had told him about Hansen and the three boys. The judge ruled that John would not take the stand because of the Federal Supremacy Act. John was retired, but the FBI didn't want him on the stand at all.

It is safe to say that the defense had its own, new problems. Professor Leonard Goodman made a fatal mistake on this case. He used his students to gather and collect any of the information that pertained to the case. He spread all of his reports and findings across his table in a rather disorderly manner.

Another crucial mistake was Mark Hansen, Ken's youngest son. He didn't show up for this trial to perjure himself like he had in the previous trial. This was in direct contrast to Danny Hansen, who refused to show up for the first trial even after being subpoenaed, by his father's attorney.

With good reason, Danny was never prosecuted for the offense. Compounding their dilemma was the absence of Frank Jayne, who had passed away and could not tell his version of Ken Hansen's earlier years.

We were now in the ceremonial courtroom with its larger seating capacity. The first witness was called upon to give testimony. After her part had concluded, I took the witness stand. Tom Biesty was now serving as the lead prosecutor for the State.

I was sworn in, and the prosecution was very satisfied with my brief but accurate testimony. Now it was time for the cross examination by Hansen's defense attorney, Goodman.

The first few questions were basic, common-knowledge questions that everyone present knew regarding the answers. Then, for some reason which I will never know, he asked me a question that he didn't know the answer to. I kept on answering the question like it was a Johnny Carson monologue. I went on for about five minutes, all while he rifled through stacks of documents looking for an answer to impeach me, as a witness.

He continued this bizarre approach, asking me a question he didn't know the answer to, and then looking through his notes, over and over, revealing himself to be both incompetent and inept, in my eyes.

He asked me about Curt Hansen and his relationship with me, about when I had first met Kenny, and when I had first conversed with him about the murdered boys. He never raised a single objection to any one of my many statements.

Again, my best guess on his court tactic and strategy was that he was looking through his notes for records that could impeach me, as a witness— but I knew the facts and wasn't about to lie: I didn't have to. When you tell the truth, it always remains the truth and is easy to remember. Sometimes when people lie, they can't remember the lie that they told. That was no concern for me, and I have court transcripts to prove it.

My cross examination lasted several hours. I should reiterate that Goodman never once raised any objections even though some of my testimony had nothing to do with the facts of the case. When I was through with my cross examination, I assure you it didn't help with Hansen's defense.

As usual, I had looked directly at the jurors faces, one by one, and took in their reactions as I spoke. Their body language told me that they were disgusted with this line of questioning. I also looked at the prosecution team and couldn't help but notice the grin on Scott Cassidy's face.

As I wrapped up my testimony, the judge asked me to step down from the witness stand. I returned to the witness room with the several other witnesses, who were waiting their turn to testify.

John Rotunno approached me and asked me, "How do you do that? You were so calm and collected. He didn't rattle you at all. I wish I could do that!"

I really didn't think what I had done was a big deal because I had simply told him the truth. I remained there in the witness room until all of the prosecution's witnesses had testified for that day.

I returned to my hotel, packed up my belongings, and headed out for home. Later, as I watched the news from my house, I learned that Hansen was convicted a second time. I also saw Beatrice Blane, the aunt of the Schuessler boys who had been murdered, on WGN. She said that she had been waiting a long time for this and that justice had been served. She hoped that Hansen suffered for a long time in prison. I received several calls of gratitude and appreciation for my involvement in the case.

The only thing that gave me concern in this case were the questions about the money that I had received from the ATF. There were thousands of dollars spent on the trial for phone calls, locating services, transportation, and various other things which gave me no personal gain. I had signed numerous receipts for each expenditure. What's more, I was never compensated for my time and services.

I did, however, and without prior knowledge, receive a reward from the first trial. At the time it was given to me, I had no financial need for the reward money—but I did take it because the agents had worked so hard on providing it to me. I was genuinely thankful for their expression and efforts. If money had ever been my motivation for getting involved in my work undercover, then I can assure you I have been paid far less than even half the $1.60 per hour federal minimum-wage standard that was present when I began offering my service back in 1971.

I kept track of Kenneth Hansen in the Pontiac State Prison. The day he died, I notified Tom Biesty and United Press International. All of the publicity regarding his public trials were of a large magnitude and received a great deal of media coverage. His death was a ten second segment on the news and three lines in UPI. I thought my run as a trial witness was finally over, but little did I know that Mitch Mars would be calling upon me only a few months later to help out in the Operation Family Secrets trial.

THE INCEPTION OF
"OPERATION FAMILY SECRETS"

I had left Chicago and ended my tenure as an FBI mole, as they termed it, on September 15th, 1988, after the arrest of Frank "The German" Schweihs. Sometime later I got a call from Tom Moriarty, a former Criminal Intelligence Division agent for the Internal Revenue Service, working for the United States Justice Department. We frequently spoke to each other after I had left town as he was a trusted friend of mine. From time to time he would ask me for help, and I usually obliged.

Tom would meet me at the airport near my home, and we would fly into Chicago's O'Hare Airport where agents would pick me up and bring me down to the United States Attorney's office, under some very heavy security protocols. When I say very heavy security, I'm talkin' very heavy security!

Let me paint a picture here for you of my first visit. We walked towards the concourse exiting the plane. Tom told me to walk about four feet ahead of him while he relayed directions on which way to turn as we came to any junctions. This came as a surprise to me because we had been seated for the entire flight together, but he now wanted to distance himself from me. He was wearing a white trench coat and began talking into his sleeve. I soon noticed there were other people on all sides of the terminal that were staged there surrounding us to keep pace with me as we went to the "Departures" entrance rather than "Arrivals."

When we exited the airport, passing through the large sliding glass doors, I was shocked to see that there was nobody there! I was used to seeing hundreds of people around that area in one of the busiest airports on earth, but the place looked like a ghost town. No Chicago police or anything were present. I kind of felt like I was in on the set of some post-apocalyptic sci-fi movie or something.

The police had placed barricades on the entrance ramps, I was told, as a four-door sedan pulled up. Tom opened the door and told me to get in. It was an unmarked FBI car. On the ramp leading to the exit points of the airport, two cars rolled up in front of us and several cars came in from the rear while we made our way out to the Kennedy Expressway. All of this was very strange to me. Tom never told me what was planned to transport me—and this was all unexpected and very overwhelming.

I eventually became used to these proceedings and the elaborate protection that was in place throughout my repeated returns to Chicago to help give my input on their gathered intelligence. They would ask me to identify photographs and wiretap transcripts with blotted out names. I was basically a consultant for them.

One of my visits included a trip to a building where some "Joker Poker" video machines were housed. I knew they were seized from the Outfit. It reminded me of how they had tried to muscle in on my old store and install one there over my insistence that they were not authorized to do so. They packed it back up, and I never heard another word from anyone about them again—until federal authorities confiscated them and took possession of them from other locations. A lot of the time I had an inside knowledge of things like this, but other queries they made to me were either too recent for me to know about or had nothing to do with me so I couldn't be of assistance. After concluding my visits with Tom, I was typically dropped off at the O'Hare Airport and a member of Tom's team kept visual contact with me until I got on my red-eye flight back home.

* * *

In 2002, Tom left me a message on my answering machine to give him a call. I got back to him some time later, and after about an hour of small talk, he asked me if I would give Mitch Mars, a Strike Force Assistant U.S. Attorney, a call. I asked why Mitch, whom I had known since the early 1980s, didn't give me a call himself.

"Red, he can't do that," Tom told me. "You have to contact him because of your status."

I was curious and hesitant to approach him without knowing what he wanted. After a long debate with Tom, I decided to make the call.

A few days later I reached out to Mitch Mars by telephone. We chatted for a while asking each other how and what we were doing.

I finally asked him, "Why did Tom ask me to give you a call?"

He told me that Tom was his only way of contacting me and that he couldn't do it himself.

"What da ya need, Mitch?"

He told me that he was putting together a case that he needed my help with since it was targeting multiple Outfit figures. Little did I know that this was going to be the largest organized crime trial in the history of the Chicago Outfit.

"But what do ya need from me, Mitch?"

He told me that it was important and that he needed my help doing a few things that only I could do for their investigation. At that point, he asked me if I would meet with two of his chief investigators. They could fly out so we would meet in person.

"Mitch, please don't tell me that your investigators are FBI agents," I said, with a sickening feeling welling up in my stomach.

"Why would you say that?"

Both Tom and Mitch knew that I had a long history with the FBI. I told him that I simply didn't get along well with them. After the last trial that they had involved me in, I wasn't happy with things. They got what they needed from me, and I was still battling with them regarding unfulfilled promises that they had made to me. He convinced me that his investigators were hand-picked, and he repeatedly assured me that I would have no problems with them, whatsoever. I agreed to give it a try and meet with the agents.

Several weeks later, Ted MacNamara and Chris Mackey, both young FBI agents, met me at a local hotel. They declined my offer to come to my home which was fine by me.

Over the course of a few days, we visited the typical places hotel patrons would frequent as we talked about a lot of things. I was shown a few pictures of Outfit guys. I knew some of them who I readily identified but some I simply couldn't place because their faces were new to me. After all, this was 2002, and I had left Chicago back in 1988. The structure and players of the Outfit had changed dramatically.

The agents seemed to be pleased with me and my responses. They were very friendly throughout our daily visits. I would return to my place each evening while they would prepare for the next day. When the visit concluded, we parted company and they returned to Chicago.

Sometime later Mitch flew out with them and told me the whole story of how he thought the trial was going to play out. He wanted me to take the stand while he showed some video footage to the court. The videotapes were made by me, in my apartment, in the late 1980s and featured recordings of Frank Schweihs discussing details of Outfit figures, several homicides, and other unlawful ventures.

He wanted to ask me about some of the things on the tapes to make sure I could still remember them so that things would be clear while we discussed them in front of the jury. It gave him great confidence to know that I could still confirm, authenticate, and help interpret my recordings with spot-on accuracy. At that time, he didn't have a very good copy of the first trial transcripts of Frank Schweihs because his were moldy from not being kept in a safe and dry storage location.

I left the hotel to return home, and I came back with a surprise for him. I was able to give him a fresh copy of the original transcripts of Frank's first trial, a copy that Tom Knight had given to me right after the trial had concluded, from 1989. After showing them to him the following day, all three of the agents gathered around to inspect them and Mitch said, "This is gonna make it a whole lot easier!"

His copies simply weren't adequate to fulfill his goals. Ted McNamara was impressed with the condition of the documents, and Mitch was amazed that I had them in the first place.

At that time, I was told that the videotapes I had made for the FBI, in their entirety, would *never* be shown. Only the specific excerpts that Mitch planned to use would be viewable in the courtroom. They weren't going to use the parts of the tapes that included Louie "the Mooch" Eboli, or other sorted mob figures.

I had approximately one hundred hours or more of conversation footage, audio and video, that I had collected over the course of eighteen months for the FBI. I was told only a select few minutes would be used for this case, and they needed my testimony to be able to corroborate what was said on those recordings.

They left the following day, and Mitch asked if it would be okay if he or the members on his team contacted me. I told him that would be fine as long as it was limited to him, Ted or Chris. He agreed to that arrangement, and we parted ways.

The forty-three-page indictment came down in April of 2005. Several of the defendants hired attorneys and worked towards a plea bargain instead of an actual trial. After all, they were guilty, and everyone knew it. Chris kept in contact with me regarding updates and developments of the upcoming trial while the FBI made the arrests—at least most of the arrests. Two key defendants were nowhere to be found and were on the run or in hiding. This caused a significant delay.

BACK TO THE WINDY CITY

So it was off to Chicago, for the Family Secrets trial, right?

Ya right! I got a call from agent Mackey who told me, "Joey Lombardo and Frank Schweihs are on the lam," which is a law enforcement/mobster term for ducking the police to avoid arrest.

Schweihs and Lombardo had seen, through news media coverage, that there was a warrant for their arrests and went into hiding to avoid prosecution. It took several months and a $10,000 reward offer [by the FBI] for tips leading to the arrest of each of the fugitives. Eventually, they got the leads and help needed to capture Frank "The German" Schweihs in Berea, Kentucky, on December 16, 2005.

The landlord of the place that Frankie was staying at recognized him as the guy featured in the news and called his local FBI to claim the reward. FBI agents immediately left Chicago to investigate, and, after several hours of detailed surveillance, they picked him up off of the street as he was going to the grocery store. He didn't resist arrest and was taken into government custody without incident. The landlord received his $10,000 reward. Authorities drove Frank straight to Chicago, passing the very cemetery where Eugenia Pappas, a former girlfriend who he had allegedly murdered back in 1962, was buried.

Frank was formally booked and fingerprinted at the MCC [Metropolitan Correctional Center] in downtown Chicago, to await his forthcoming trial. Naturally, he was held without bond, as a flight risk defendant. This was only the second time in his life he was held without bond, the first being after his September 15th, 1988, arrest. I'm sure he was upset about it on both occasions and resented the fact that he ever became involved with me.

While all of this was going on with Frank, a cat and mouse game ensued with Joey. The reward for his capture was increased to $20,000, as he was the final guy they needed for the trial to proceed. Joey Lombardo constantly sent letters to his attorney to give to the judge who had been assigned the case, the honorable James Zagel. He would mail them to his attorney, Rick Halprin, from various public mailboxes that bore Chicago postmarks, in order to avoid giving up his location in the suburbs. Halprin, in turn, would present each letter to the judge. It was all an attempt to secure a separate trial for himself.

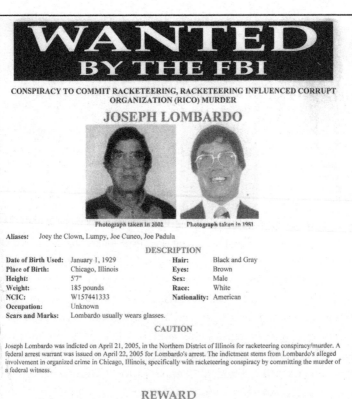

Wanted Poster Joey Lombardo (Courtesy of John Drummond)

Lombardo didn't want to be tried with the other crime figures as he was sure that his association with such affiliates would make it less likely for him to beat the charges that had been filed against him. Those charges included the bold, deliberate, daytime murder of Danny Seifert, along with several other murders, racketeering, shake-downs, implicating him as a ringleader. When the FBI puts up twenty grand, you know someone is going to drop a dime on them!

Judge Zagel refused all of the motions. The envelopes, which Joey had sent his letters in, were confiscated in an effort to capture him. Chris had called me and told me that they were confident that Joey was not in the Bahamas, as I was concerned that he would flee there.

Joey had some dental problems and went to see Dr. Pasquale [Pat] Spilatro, Jr., for treatment in his Park Ridge, Illinois office. Pat was the elder brother of Anthony and Michael Spilatro, known Las Vegas mob guys who were murdered by their peers while Joey was away doing some time in federal prison. Dr. Spilatro, after several visits and earning the trust of Joey, learned the location of his hideout.

Pat later testified that one of the things that he had asked Joey, in his several dental visits, was if his brothers would have been murdered if Joey had been a free man at that time.

"No, it never would have happened had I been out," Joey told him.

Dr. Spilatro later contacted an FBI agent with the details of Joey's whereabouts, and not long after Frankie's transport, Joey "The Clown" Lombardo was taken into custody. It took place in the very early hours of January 13th, 2006, in an alley of Elmwood Park, a Chicago suburb. Joey was also arrested without incident and taken directly to the MCC for processing. Even though Dr. Spilatro ran a very successful dental practice as an oral surgeon, he still graciously accepted the FBI's $20,000 reward check.

Agent Mackey and I had been in contact by telephone throughout the aforementioned events. He called me to inform me of the fact that they had captured Joey and told me that he was personally there when he was apprehended. Now he made plans to fly me into Chicago to be present for the judicial proceedings.

Several months before the court case, I was checked into a hotel in the Chicago suburbs under the protection and care of the FBI. Chris Mackey, in his inexperience, walked me up to the hotel desk and expected me to use my own credit card, under my own name and information, to check into the hotel room, all while hotel surveillance cameras were running.

I took him onto the side and told him, "No way am I going to do this!"

He asked me, "So what do you want me to do?"

"Use your credit card and put the room under your name." I told him.

"Why, Red, you know you're going to be reimbursed for it anyway!" came his reply.

"This is for MY security and this is how other agents have done it in the past."

He then confirmed that would be okay and checked in while I claimed "his room" for myself. We thus avoided a potential compromise in my location while I was in Chicago, preparing for the upcoming trial.

Joey Lombardo, 2006 Mugshot

THE DAILY GRIND

Every day, early in the morning, agents would pick me up and drive me to the Federal Building where I would see Tom Moriarty, Mitch Mars, John Scully, and a new member of the office team, T. Markus Funk. I also met and talked to several other agents on the case who were unfamiliar to me, including Mike Maseth.

The pre-trial motions were going on every single day. I was told by federal representatives who worked this case that several of the defendants would plead guilty once they knew I was going to be testifying, leaving only the final five to stand trial—or so I thought.

Mitch had told me that they intended on calling Frank Cullotta as a witness for the prosecution, as Cullotta was on the witness list. After a long and heated discussion about Cullotta's credibility and the fact that he had told Mitch he planned on writing a book about the trial, Mitch agreed not to put him on the witness stand.

After all, Frank Cullotta had already written several books about his activities with the Chicago Outfit, including the murders that he had personally committed. I was shocked that he was being considered to testify and told Mitch, "He is full of bullshit." Mitch agreed with me on that point and Frank was never called to testify, although television news media had reported that he would be on the witness list.

One U.S. Marshal, John T. Ambrose, part of the security team charged with the transport of trial witnesses, was tried some time later for leaking information about the case to the Chicago Outfit. John Ambrose's father, a former Chicago police officer, was in prison with several other Outfit associates, and he had put them in contact with his son. He told them about a secret location, the "safe house", where several people were going to be kept during the trial, and included their locations and the times they were scheduled for transport to and from the courthouse.

The would-be residents of that safe house were all in the witness protection program. Upon hearing of this leak, a former Outfit associate, Alva Johnson "Johnny" Rodgers, refused to go to the safe house. Where they kept him or any of the other witnesses for that matter, remains a secret to this day. Later on, U.S. Marshal Ambrose was tried and convicted of this crime. The judge in his case was less than sympathetic towards his actions and his sentencing matched those sentiments.

THE ATTACK

These guys worked from dawn to dusk every day. Agent Chris Mackey and I joined them every morning as he transported me to the Everett McKinley Dirksen U.S. Courthouse building. After arriving there each day, I was not allowed to go off the floor they assigned me, much less leave the building. Even eating lunch was a problem because I was not allowed to go to the cafeteria or any other place to get something to eat, for fear of someone recognizing me. This meant that by the time I was taken back to the hotel every evening, I was practically starving.

This created a problem with the anxiety medication I had been taking since 1982. It is supposed to be taken with a meal and should be administered on a regular schedule, three set times each day. If my meds are not taken, as prescribed, it increases my adrenaline flow tenfold according to my doctor—and anything can happen. Everyone was so consumed with their own jobs that my medication became a problem, my problem, which in turn would affect them.

One night, right after Chris drove me back to the hotel where I was staying, the moment I feared most finally happened. As I walked into my room, I had a full blown panic attack. The room was spinning, and I was dizzy as I ran all around my quarters. Everything appeared to be moving and swaying in every direction, and I couldn't get my bearings. I had lost all control!

Poor Chris didn't know what to do and, looking back, I know he had never seen anything like it. This wasn't something that just randomly happened; it was because I hadn't taken my medication with meals for such a long span of time that my body chemistry was now suffering. He tried to talk to me, but I simply didn't understand anything he said. He quickly got on the phone and called for more agents to come over and help.

I recall a compelling urge to leave the building through my sealed third story picture window, as four or five agents quickly came into my room. I remember telling them what was causing my episode and how I wanted a drink of Scotch to help settle me down. Chris was not going to let me drink any whiskey at all. I think he was afraid something worse could result.

One of the guys who just arrived told me he would stay in the suite all night with me if it would help calm me down. He kept talking to me and sent another agent to get me a sandwich and I took a pill with it. The agent that had volunteered to stay with me appeared to be in his mid-thirties with a beard and tattoos which really set him apart from any FBI agent that I had ever met. I guessed that he worked undercover, wearing blue jeans and a pullover T-shirt. As we conversed, he told me about some of his undercover activities, confirming my guess.

He joked with me a bit and gave me a coin that had "Chicago FBI" on one side and "The United States Justice Department" on the other side. He was very calming and understanding and helped settle me down enough to pull me out of my anxiety attack. He sent out for a very small bottle of Dewar's Scotch, and I sat at the table with him and drank it while we talked, as the other agents eventually left the room. That was a big help! I calmed down a bit, and plans were made. Agent Mackey had gone home for the night and left me in the care of my new friends.

My sleeping arrangements were changed for that night, by authority of the FBI. The agent who stayed with me in my suite was very understanding. The rest of the guys charged with my care, the remaining five or six of them, rented a room across the hall. Some had to spend the night in sleeping bags since there were no other rooms available at the hotel on that floor. I soon fell asleep after the tranquilizing effect of the booze, medications, and calming conversation kicked in, retiring to my bed for the night.

I woke up very early the next morning and told the agents that I was ready to go for the day. I watched as a long line of agents filed out of the room across the hall. All of them appeared to have blood-shot eyes and had not spent a very restful night in their shared quarters. While they were getting roused for the day, I hit the shower. We all packed up and went away to our different destinations within a few minutes.

On that day I rode with a young, newer agent, named Dave White. He was a great guy. He tried to do anything he could to please me and make me comfortable. We stopped at his apartment in Franklin Park so he could drop off his sleeping bag that he had slept in, then we grabbed some food. He asked me where I wanted to go for lunch. We stopped at an Italian Beef restaurant. I was so happy to eat an Italian Beef! After the meal, he reminded me to take my pill and accompanied me down to the Federal Building. After my panic attack it seemed that the agents responsible for my care became more attentive to my needs and made sure I had food and my medication at the scheduled times each day. I was very appreciative.

All of these guys were great men, even Chris—he was just too busy with the case to focus on what I needed at that time—and I am sure he was caught off guard. We adjusted my eating habits, and I did not suffer from another episode for the rest of the days that led up to the trial. I was now in a regular daily habit of going back and forth from the hotel to the offices downtown.

My Day in Court

After opening statements by both the prosecutors and defense attorneys, my day finally arrived. It was time for me to take the stand. It was a Tuesday and I was dressed in a suit, as usual. Five FBI agents with radios and earpieces walked me up and down several staircases, then through some long hallways up to a door that opened into yet another hallway. That corridor was filled with newsmen and spectators.

John "Bulldog" Drummond, from Chicago's CBS News, and I smiled at each other as agents stepped between us in the hallway to the courtroom. He said "hi" to me. I would have liked to have talked to him, but an agent got between us as they hurriedly walked me down through the crowds and into the courtroom entrance.

I had known John for many years and had provided him with information on pieces he would air in his newscasts. He did an exclusive interview with me shortly after Frank Schweihs's first conviction, at an undisclosed location around 1990. It aired many times on CBS under the title "Confessions of a Mob Informant." Later, I provided him with key information on the Peterson-Schuessler Murders that were exclusive to him and his CBS station, where he worked. He always referred to me as "an anonymous source."

We developed a very good relationship over the years, and I was always impressed with his willingness to focus on the facts and not offer opinions that would slant things one way. He seemed to be a very fair reporter, and he would not give up his sources to anyone. Prior to the trial, John had written and published two books that covered his years of reporting and made mention of me in both of them—even devoting an entire chapter to me in his first book, *Thirty Years in the Trenches*.

It had taken three weeks to select that jury. Judge Zagel had decided to give each juror a number instead of using their names as he personally asked them the questions to see if they were qualified to be jurors in this case. He wanted to assure them that they would be safe from any retribution or bribery attempts. The defense attorneys were not permitted to de voyeur, as in a normal trial. The defense attorneys protested but all to no avail. Judge Zagel was firm on that decision.

It was finally time for me to testify to the court. As I stepped up to the witness stand, I looked at all of the wires from the electronic equipment, the spectator gallery, and the jury that was seated in the room.

I swore to tell the whole truth as I took my place on the witness stand. I surveyed the courtroom and could see a special section for the press representatives and other VIPs such as organized crime victims' family members. Looking over at the defendants and their army of attorneys, I could plainly see this was a bigger case than I had thought it would be. I also saw the several video monitors that would later play proceedings for the jury and the rest of the courtroom, myself included, along with the wiring for the many headphones that would provide the audio tracks from the tapes. Some tapes were played that were audio-only files.

I saw a colorful man dressed in a pink suit with pink socks to match, a fact that he proudly displayed to the many media reporters who were present. This short and squatty man who made a spectacle of himself was Frank Calabrese, Sr.'s attorney, Joe "The Shark" Lopez.

I saw a mixed group of people in the jury box, on my right. Those people really stood out to me as they were to be referred to by the numbers readily visible on the front of their shirts, instead of using their proper names, as in other trials I had attended. This was all in an effort to keep them safe and untainted by the proceedings. They appeared to me to be just everyday, average people who were very alert but dressed casually. I glanced over at Judge Zagel in his black robe with his grey wavy hair that had been neatly trimmed. He looked very distinguished, and I could tell he was a no-nonsense judge, by his demeanor, and that he was here for the trial and not for the spectacle.

The courtroom was packed with people and electronic equipment, along with FBI agents to help with the trial's proceedings to make sure the equipment was working properly for those who needed it. I had to literally watch each step as I made my way to the witness stand, so as to avoid stepping on and possibly disconnecting or damaging one of the many cords that blanketed the floor. The floor was carpeted and duct tape was pieced together to cover the cords and keep the many connecting wires in place. This was all an effort to make the video and audio evidence readily accessible to everyone who needed to review it. I was also impressed with the fact that each exhibit was queued up and ready to go. The thought that went behind this highly technical presentation was considerable, and it showed.

Spectators had to take a number to be seated. If they left their spectator seat for any reason, there was another person waiting in line to fill it. It looked like a real circus to me, and I had never seen or heard of anything like it before in my life. It was like a line for free beer at Wrigley Field on a hot summer playoff day.

Mitch Mars began by asking me a few questions, including my name. His initial questions were short and direct and only required a yes or no from me. I faced the jury, to my right, when I answered the questions that he posed.

As I recall, his questions were pretty typical for a trial of this nature. He asked me if I knew what a street tax was and if I'd ever paid it. He then asked me to describe it. I told him I was required to pay a street tax to open and stay in business.

"Basically it's a permission to be in a business without being hurt by someone or possibly being burned down. I was not looking forward to have an accident—as accidents by Frank's definition always meant murder."

While I answered his questions, I was specifically thinking of Paul Gonsky, who Frankie had murdered, and a guy named Leslie that I had heard about that had his place blow up and, after rebuilding it, was murdered because he didn't comply with the wishes of the Outfit. "It was expected. If you didn't pay, you might have a problem!"

Mitch Mars presented an old mugshot of Joey Lombardo to me and the court and asked if I could see him. Joey stood up, a frail specimen of a man—not like I had seen him last—and I chuckled as I looked at him in a baggy, expensive suit that hung on him like it was four sizes too big.

"That's him standing over there" [as he stood up] "but he looked a lot better then than he does now."

Joey didn't react much to my comments, and he just smiled and resumed his seat. The jury and spectators laughed as I said it. Mitch quickly proceeded with another question.

The prosecution secured cordless headphones for each of the jurors, and they made sure everyone's were working properly before they began playing videotapes on several monitors, television screens, and a couple of big screens so that everyone in the courtroom could watch the exhibit. They brought me a laptop and headphones while they played excerpts of some of the videotapes that I had made of me talking to Frank Schweihs, back in 1987 and 1988.

From time to time they would stop the tapes, and Mitch Mars would ask me more questions to help authenticate and explain what had unfolded in each scene. I was constantly keeping eye contact with the jury as I answered the questions that he had for me. All of Mitch's questions pertained to the tapes, both before and after they were shown to the jury. Once jurors had seen the video evidence, it seemed that they all were very attuned to my words and explanations, as later reported by Muriel Clair of Chicago's WGN TV.

I remember a specific moment as the videotape recording played. I had been instructed by my FBI Handler to try and get Frank to think someone was coming around bothering me and asking questions about who owned the place. I fabricated a story to Frank, and he went for it and got increasingly upset about my report.

Frank was trying to figure out who it was that would have the gall to do it. He wondered if it was an undercover cop or maybe Mike Glitta, the ambitious Rush Street Crew operator who was trying to expand his territory.

Schweihs said, on tape, "What does he think, just because Lombo's away, things have changed? He knows better than that! And I don't think he'd be that stupid to try and step on my fuckin' prick or the people I'm affiliated with! Do you understand? So this jagoff that comes here has to be some fuckin' half ass wiseguy that's just goin' round tryin' to arm joints. I don't know what we're gonna do: we might have to make a believer outta him."

"Couldn't it be somebody that supplied his store?" I said, trying to imply that a Cleveland family might be to blame.

Frank responded, "They'd get their ass knocked off, Red, they know that. Chicago's got the worst reputation in the United States. Even them fuckin' New Yorkers don't want to come around here and fuck around! No one would win a battle with the Grand Avenue Crew, and there's no one's that has the right to come in and fuck in our domain. This is a declared fuckin joint, and nobody's got the right to fuck with ya's. I don't care if it's Al Capone's brother reincarnated!"

Also adding, "You're with me, and I don't think that anyone would try to step on my fucking prick. Remember, you're with me, and I don't think anybody would try and knock me down or any of the people that I am affiliated with. I'm a hard guy to knock down and you're with me! They gotta go through me to get to you, nobody's gonna fuck with ya's. You've got my solemn promise on that!"

The media later capitalized on the reference to Al Capone and even displayed his picture in the story that recapped the proceedings of that day in court, but I knew that Frankie was actually referring to Ralph Capone. Ralph had run his own territory on the South Side of Chicago, being a one-time boss of the Outfit. His territory was out in Hickory Hills and Willow Springs. He had been a long time associate of the area that Joey and Frank oversaw at the time the tapes were made. All of this was said in Frank's effort to adamantly prove he had the power and muscle to do what he said.

Some of the jurors were taking copious notes during my testimony, on the spiral notebooks that the court had provided them with and others stopped and set them down as they watched Frankie Schweihs go into his furious rage. One lady juror, with dark brown hair, looked at me several times as she wrote on her notebook. I remember asking myself, "What is she writing?" I looked into each jurors' eyes, whenever I could, all while answering Mitch's questions. I could clearly see each of their assigned numbers on their shirts or blouses. As things proceeded, I felt confident that my testimony was convincing, but I knew the tapes were even more convincing than my words.

After other questions about the videos and audiotapes, Mitch concluded by asking me: "And were you afraid at that time?"

I paused as I thought over his question and then said, "Yes."

"What were you afraid of?"

"I feared death!"

The courtroom was tense and anxiously awaiting each of my answers. It seemed to me that my closing remarks supported the statements that Frankie had previously asserted on videotape. Those were my final words in my testimony for the prosecution.

It took a bit of time to go through everything that we had needed to address but we finally wrapped things up as Judge Zagel recessed for the following day right after my testimony was finished. The judge dismissed the jury for an adjournment, and a number of the jurors made eye contact with me as they passed the witness stand on the way to leave the courtroom. I felt I had connected with them.

I left the courtroom, knowing that the next day I would be cross examined by Rick Halprin, Joey Lombardo's attorney. He was the only attorney that wanted to question me, of all the many attorneys on the massive team for the defense. It seemed to me, at the time, that nobody wanted to touch my testimony with a ten foot pole. I suppose they had bigger fish to fry with other witnesses.

Judge Zagel issued a gag order regarding the case and forbade Halprin, Lombardo's attorney, from answering any media questions about what he would or would not question me about on the following day. It was noted by various television reporters as Halprin refused to comment regarding questions relating to my testimony.

Attorney Rick Halprin

A representative from the FBI was featured on the news and said, "It's one thing to have a witness testify from his recollection. In this case, the tapes told it all, out of the defendant's mouth! The tapes made the case."

The following morning Halprin did his cross examination. Rick Halprin asked me if I ever put money into his defendant's hand.

I answered, "No."

He asked me where I had met his client, and I replied, "At American Bonding, on State Street. I believe the building was owned by Joey Cosentino."

This upset him because American Bonding was a known meeting place for such people as Frank Schweihs, Joey Lombardo, Irwin Weiner, Tony Spilatro, and other underworld figures. He then asked me how I ended up at American Bonding and I told him that I was introduced to his client there by Curt Hansen, during the Weenie World Scandal. He asked me what year it was, along with several other questions that he fired off in rapid succession.

Mitch Mars objected several times, and Judge Zagel upheld each of his objections. Judge Zagel admonished him, telling him to move on with his questioning. Halprin knew he was in a tough spot so he kept trying to raise questions that he could use to try and impeach my testimony.

Halprin began to ask me if this was the only case that I had ever testified in, and I answered, "No, this is the second one in federal court."

He asked me what other trials I had testified in, and I paused as Mitch Mars objected to his question. He then asked me how many times I had been to American Bonding and to describe it to the court and to the jurors, placing a hand-drawn diagram in front of me.

I told him I didn't recall how many times I was there, but the thing that stood out the most was a large easel that was used to account for the scim money that came in from Circus Circus Casino Hotel in Las Vegas. He quickly asked me where the easel was [on his hand-drawn diagram of American Bonding] and to point to it. He also asked me where Tony Spilatro's office was and to point to that, all in an obvious attempt to impeach my testimony.

Mitch objected to his rapid line of questioning, and Judge Zagel sustained it. At one time, he asked me about testifying in state court, and Mitch objected to that also, with Judge Zagel again sustaining his objection, saying, "It has no relevance. Move on!"

Halprin's strategy appeared to be a lame effort to gain sympathy or cause doubt in the minds of the jurors, but the videotapes had already told the real story. They gave an inside view of how the Outfit did whatever they wanted to do and how they felt about their position, their power, and their influence over others.

After the cross examination was complete, I was taken back to my hotel room. The FBI agents who drove me there told me that Alva Johnson Rodgers AKA Johnny Rodgers took the stand right after me and corroborated everything in my testimony, adding a conversation between himself and Lombardo regarding Danny Seifert.

Rodgers testified that Lombardo told him, "We're never gonna see that piece of shit again!" [referring to Danny Seifert]. To that point, the case had gone exactly as expected by the prosecution.

Skipping Town

A waiting me in my hotel room were two agents who I had never previously met. One was a male, and the other was a female. They waited while I gathered my things, and we then left the hotel together, headed out of town. We waited for hours on end at the airport, in the VIP lounge that the female agent had a pass for. We were trying to get a standby seat on any open flight that would return me to my home.

Flight after flight passed us by without any vacancies until we finally got seated in a 727. Because all of the pilots qualified to fly the 727 had filled their logbooks, by FAA regulations, they could not fly so we had to walk back through the terminal concourse and into the terminal itself. At that time, I was thinking, "What idiot made these travel arrangements that this female agent is defending?" We were screwed!

My biological pattern was once more upset after such a long and stress-filled day without food or medication. I think all of us were filled with disgust when we heard, at about 1:00 a.m., that there were no more flights leaving until the following morning. We were all dead tired. The male agent had a look of genuine disgust on his face as the two FBI agents discussed what to do. I had been awake since 6:00 a.m. and it was now almost 2:00 a.m.

My protecting agents decided we should go to a hotel, back in downtown Chicago, and try to sleep for three hours or so. This is something that I had no intentions of doing. Before I had taken this trip, I had called a friend who told me that if I had any troubles, then I should give him a call and I could stay at his place in Indiana. That was just what I had in my mind when I hailed a taxi.

As we walked out of the airport they were looking for a rental car, and I was looking for a cab. The male agent pleaded for me to wait, and I just walked away as the female told the male agent, "Let him go. I've had enough!"

I got in a cab and went to light up a cigarette when the driver told me that smoking was not allowed in his cab. I got out, and the male agent made several attempts, by stopping people, to ask for a light for my cigarette. The reason I didn't have one for myself was the fact that my checked baggage had long-since departed on the original flight which had been overbooked. This left me with nothing, but the clothes on my back—a fact that was somewhat annoying to me.

We eventually drove a rental car to a hotel back downtown and checked in for the night. I really needed some food. They ordered a pizza so that I could take my medications on a full stomach. As we sat in my room waiting for the delivery guy, the female agent told me, "You know we're doing you a favor, and you should be grateful!"

That's when we had some words regarding who was actually doing the favor for whom. There was no way Mitch Mars could ever make me testify, unless I wanted to, and I sure let her know it. Things got quiet after that exchange and the pizza finally arrived. I got some dinner and took my medication before retiring for the nap. Both of the agents also retired to their own rooms.

I slept two hours, and it was time to leave. We all checked out of the hotel and went to Midway airport, under the hopes that there would be some vacancies on a morning flight. They swapped agents for me again— except for the female. The agent that had given me the FBI coin and had previously stayed with me in my hotel room on the night of my panic attack became a part of my replacement escort. I figured that whoever was in charge thought that this would make it easier to return me to my home.

A flight was available, and he sat next to me in the 737 jet. He told me that he was retired from service with the Air Force. We talked freely as the plane flew me home, and he, once again, gave me great comfort. He was a great guy, as all of the agents I met were, with the exception of the female agent with the attitude. As I tried to figure out what had made her so unpleasant towards me, I recall thinking, "She must be trying to stand out better than the male FBI agents. It's probably just a gender thing."

Whatever the reason, I was glad when we landed and relieved after I found my luggage, although I had to find it at the other terminal used for the original flight which had been provided by another airline company. I loaded it into the large SUV with blackened windows that they were using to transport me home.

When we arrived at my house, I was not allowed to exit the SUV until a full perimeter search was conducted, at the insistence of the female agent. She told me to give her my house keys and to provide her with the security code for my alarm so that they could secure the house before I entered.

They proceeded to inspect each room, and after they had gone through my entire house, pistols drawn, they let me in. I came into my house and found my keys on the kitchen table. My house had been vacant for nearly a month so I turned on the air conditioning for some fresh, cool air and closed my garage door, as I told them, "Bye!" They were already on their way out of my driveway, with the female agent at the wheel. I am sure we were both glad to be rid of each other. Things were over, and I was finally home and back to my life as an average U.S. citizen.

The Family Secrets trial eventually concluded on August 30th, 2007. All fourteen defendants were convicted on various charges and over eighteen murders had been solved. The trial lasted a long time, but Mitch Mars and John Scully made it happen, along with the help of Markus Funk, FBI agents Chris Mackey, Ted MacNamara, Mike Maseth, and who-knows-how-many other FBI agents. The largest organized crime trial in U.S. history was now complete.

When it was all over and done, Mitch Mars passed away just a few months later from lung cancer. He was only fifty-five years old, had never smoked a day in his life, and had worked his entire career in a smoke free environment. Who would think that would happen to such a great man?

John Scully retired the very next day and became a judge in Lake County, Illinois.

T. Markus Funk left to become a partner in a high end law firm after threats were made on his life, and he was given round the clock U.S. Marshall Protection. Later, it was learned by the FBI, that, indeed, a plot was made to assassinate him.

As I look back, I really miss those guys! They wanted me to help them, but they helped me see that you really can make a difference, as long as you are willing to get involved and do what needs to be done.

THE ONE FIGHT THAT FRANK COULDN'T WIN

Frank Schweihs did not make it to the Family Secrets trial because of his ongoing battle with cancer. Judge Zagel planned on him going to trial once he was healthy enough to help represent himself, in his own defense. I imagine he figured that it would take less than a year for him to recover, but I thought differently. Frank had shown me a lump on his neck in 1987, and we had even captured the moment on videotape in my apartment. After a trip to the Mayo Clinic for treatment, he returned to tell me, as he pointed to the back of his neck, "I just bought myself ten years, son. They took the cancer out."

Later on, in 1989, he was not there for his sentencing when he was convicted of shaking me down. His prostate cancer kept him from the courtroom, as he was recovering from surgery. A few months after that, it was cancer of the colon and kidneys. They had to operate on that, too. Next it was lymphatic cancer that kept him from the courthouse. Finally, it was brain cancer. His body and then his mind were literally riddled with cancer. Nearly a year after the Family Secrets trial had concluded, on July 23, 2008, he succumbed.

It reminds me of the many conversations I had with mobsters and FBI agents alike regarding the unusually high incident rates of cancer among mob guys who spent years in prisons. They all seemed to end up with the disease after doing any significant time there.

With the passing of Frank Schweihs, no one would ever know the full report of how many people he had murdered at the bequest of others or of his own volition. No one would ever know about his side of the involvement in the murder of fellow mobster, Anthony Spilatro. No one would ever know his side of the story relating to Don Aronow, the CIA-connected speedboat tycoon who was a close personal friend and associate of former President George Herbert Walker Bush. No one would ever know his version of the events involving his fatal shooting of Danny Seifert, the young man involved in the scim of the Teamster's Pension Fund loan to build Circus Circus Hotel and Casino in Las Vegas. The public would never learn the entire process of how it had been secured through Jimmy Hoffa. Nor would they know about his role in the murder of Allen Dorfman, the man who helped secure the loan from the Teamsters Pension Fund. His possible involvement in the death of Marilyn Monroe would also remain a mystery, despite several reports that tagged him as the number one suspect in her unusual demise.

Sure, there were books written that detailed some of these events such as Milo Speriglio's *Crypt 33*, which outlines the murder details of Marilyn Monroe, as given to him by a Pappas family member. Eugena Pappas, a former girlfriend of Frank's at the time of Marilyn's death, had been found dead in the Chicago River from to a gunshot wound to the chest.

There was also *Blue Thunder*, by Thomas Burdick, that explains Frank's CIA connections to Aronow and how he was murdered. Naming Frank Schweihs as the perpetrator is different than definitively proving it within the halls of justice. So many of the cases that could have been brought against him will never come to fruition, even though they were testified to, in court.

There are just too many skeletons in his closet that will remain buried there. I am more than confident that there are countless others that I don't even know about. God only knows what secrets he took with him to the grave. Myself and many others, who dealt with him, considered as one of the most deadly and dangerous men ever to be affiliated with the Outfit. I don't know if I was fortunate or unfortunate to have learned these facts from Frank himself, but I think the public deserves to know the truth which will never be aired on television news. I don't know if I was fortunate or unfortunate to have learned these facts from Frank himself, but I think the public deserves to know the truth which will never be aired on television news.

I was told by Mitch Mars that I could never see my FBI file, even under of "The Freedom of Information Act."

In the words of Frank Schweihs, "Case closed, Moe!"

EPILOGUE

This story really isn't about my life, but about the people I interacted with, ranging from mobsters, federal agents, and other people in important positions. There are thousands of mob-related stories that I could tell you about my everyday life, in the past.

Unlike members of the news media [along with numerous attorneys] that reported their opinions, I want people to hear my side of the story, the truth, directly from the horse's mouth, so to speak. A big part of why I wrote this book was in response to the many reporters and authors who wrote things about me that just weren't true.

Another reason to write this book is to let people know that they can make a difference, if they really want to. Not everybody is able to do this, but it seems that some are capable and don't do anything about it because the risk is too great. A quote from Plato is so true:

"Justice in the life and conduct of the State is possible only as first it resides in the hearts and souls of the citizens."

Another quote by the famous politician, Henry Kissinger:

"Corrupt politicians make the other ten percent look bad."

After all, who would know better than him?

Maybe a guy who worked in concert with political figures said it best. As Joey Lombardo stated in the Family Secrets Trial:

"Politicians are the real hoodlums. There's 50 bosses in Chicago. The 50 bosses are the 50 alderman; without them you can't get anything done."

Take a good look at your own community and tell me that there isn't some sort of corruption. I believe there is corruption wherever we live, extending all the way to Washington D.C. However, it starts at a local level just like Joey explained. That's how the Chicago Outfit survives. Now that I have spelled that out, I close with my final quote from Plato:

"We can easily forgive a child who is afraid of the dark; the real tragedy of life is when men are afraid of the light."

Please make the title of this book an attitude of the past by getting involved in your community today. Prove that you do not belong to the crowd of nobodies that inspired the title of this book.

ACKNOWLEDGMENTS

First and foremost I express my sincere appreciation and thanks to my family—especially my mother, for her support and for living as long as she has. She has lived long enough to finally see how I really lived my life.

To Doc: for being such a great man. Without his help, I couldn't have lived to write this. And to his assistant George. Two of the finest people I have met in my life.

A very special thanks to my coauthor Ramon Clements and his family. Without his help, this book never would have been published. Heavenly Father above guided us, and for that I am grateful.

I also wish to acknowledge the many honest Chicago Police Officers, federal law enforcement agents and prosecutors for their hard work and dedicated efforts. I know it's a thankless job, but you still do it.

I must draw special attention to the Cook County Prosecutor's Cold Case Unit along with Scott Cassidy, the late Pat Quinn, Tom Biesty, and his investigators.

To the United States Marine Corps: my thanks for all of the training and discipline that you taught me that helped keep me alive and to the many Marines that gave their lives for our freedom. You are NOT forgotten.

I want to thank John "The Bulldog" Drummond for his example of telling the truth. After all, you were the first person to advise me to write this book. Thank you, John.

Printed in Great Britain
by Amazon

39520671R00136